IT'S NOT YOU, IT'S ME!

A CHRONIC OVERTHINKER'S GUIDE TO SELF-REFLECTION

ROSEMARY GATTUSO

HELIX PRESS

© Copyright Rosemary Gattuso

Published by: Helix Press
www.rosemarygattuso.com

All rights reserved. No part of this book may be reproduced by any mechanical, photographic, or electronic process, or in the form of a phonographic recording; nor may it be stored in a retrieval system, transmitted, or otherwise be copied for public or private use—other than for "fair use" as brief quotations embodied in articles and reviews—without prior written permission of the publisher.

The author of this book does not dispense medical advice or prescribe the use of any technique as a form of treatment for physical, emotional, or medical concerns without the advice of a physician, either directly or indirectly. The intent is to offer information of a general nature to provide the reader with a wide range of choices to help in their quest for emotional, physical, and spiritual wellbeing. Should any reader choose to make use of the information herein, this is their decision, and the contributors (and their companies), authors and publishers do not assume any responsibilities whatsoever under any conditions or circumstances. It is recommended that the reader obtain their own independent advice.

 A catalogue record for this book is available from the National Library of Australia

ISBN: 978-0-6456080-0-7

First Edition 2024

© Copyright 2024 Rosemary Gattuso
Designed and created In Australia

DEDICATION

*To Mum and Dad, this book
was only possible because of you.*

Contents

Introduction   7
Acknowledgement   10

Chapter 1: The Lacking   11
    Reflection Task One   14
    Reflection Task Two   19
    Reflection Task Three   22
    Reflection Task Four   24

Chapter 2: The Strength   27
    Reflection Task Five   28
    Reflection Task Six   33
    Reflection Task Seven   34

Chapter 3: The Evidence   37
    Reflection Task Eight   39
    Reflection Task Nine   43
    Reflection Task Ten   45
    Reflection Task Eleven   46
    Reflection Task Twelve   47
    Reflection Task Thirteen   48

Chapter 4: The Evolution of the Scales   49
    Reflection Task Fourteen   53

Chapter 5: The Scales   55
    Reflection Task Fifteen   61
    Reflection Task Sixteen   65
    Reflection Task Seventeen   70
    Reflection Task Eighteen   74
    Reflection Task Nineteen   77
    Reflection Task Twenty   81
    Reflection Task Twenty-One   86
    Reflection Task Twenty-Two   91
    Reflection Task Twenty-Three   94

Chapter 6: The Experience   97
    Reflection Task Twenty-Four   103

Chapter 7: The Scales in Practice   105
    Reflection Task Twenty-Five   108
    Meditation   109
    Visualisation—Infusion of Love   110
    Affirmations   112
    The Day in Review   113

Chapter 8: It's Not You, It's Me!   115
    Troubleshooting Guide—Comparisons   117
    Reflection Task Twenty-Six   118
    Inadmissible Evidence   119
    Reflection Task Twenty-Seven   121
    A Note About Intuition   122
    The Haunted Merry-Go-Round   123
    Reflection Task Twenty-Eight   125
    Screen Time   126
    Reflection Task Twenty-Nine   127
    Flip it to Faith   128
    Reflection Task Thirty   129
    No Regrets   130
    Eliminating The Word 'Should'   131
    Reflection Task Thirty-One   132

Bibliography   137
References   145
About The Author   150

Introduction

Challenges—those unexpected bouts of uncertainty that can infiltrate every aspect of our physical and emotional wellbeing. Instances that really push us to our capacity and question our worth.

These kinds of personal dilemmas sparked both my curiosity and self-reflection. I wanted to learn more about how people managed their daily crises and understand my own ways of tackling my day-to-day challenges. I noticed that how one person managed a blowout, compared to their neighbour being faced with the very same dilemma, could vary dramatically. This perplexed me.

My short-lived legal career—if you could call it one—served to cement the fact that the legal profession did not suit me; it did, however, introduce me to the world of mediation. An area that was considered 'alternative' by the legal world. It also saw me enter a field that moved away from 'us versus them' to 'we' and replaced blame and fault with collaboration.

When I began working as a family dispute resolution practitioner, which was essentially a complicated way of saying 'family mediator', I became the outsider who sat in, observed, and helped guide the negotiations free of judgement, opinion, or decision-making authority.

This neutral stance was almost my natural element. I often found it excruciating to make a decision or give a strong opinion when I felt mine was neither relevant nor necessary.

As a mediator, I found myself faced with families navigating the roller-coaster of change and uncertainty that often accompanied separation. Amid their grief and loss, I was able to respectfully observe and reflect on what was unfolding. At times, I caught myself triggered and personally confronted by the challenges of others, yet in the long run, I learnt more about myself than I could have imagined.

The resulting combination of my professional observations and reflection eventually led to the concepts in this book.

This role, for me, highlighted the vast differences in how people approach and manage life's challenges. It helped me see

Introduction

my patterns and ways of thinking and look at those of others around me. I noticed, more and more, that while individual circumstances varied, there were often two distinct and opposing outcomes. Did we highlight 'What's Wrong' or 'What's Strong'?

Where we place our focus could, at times, predict future responses, while also providing clues into one's lived experience.

I held these observations in my mind while, professionally, I began exploring the science behind childhood development: neuroscience. It soon became an obsession, and I found myself immersed in everything related to brain science. As the scientific underpinnings of my observations slowly revealed themselves, I moved away from categorising behaviour as 'an issue', difficult', or 'odd' to viewing everything as an 'adaptation' to one's experience.

A basic brain science perspective showed me that we are either in unsafe mode or safe mode. It's only when we are in safe mode that we can learn and function without fear. When I combined my study of child development and work as a mediator, the importance of the quality of significant relationships was continuously highlighted.

Unsafe mode seemed parallel to the 'What's Wrong' mode, and the safe mode paralleled 'What's Strong' mode.

The more these concepts churned in my head, the more I began to see representations of What's Strong and What's Wrong in every interaction, thought, emotion, and action. There were always both options. The same situation could have vastly different perspectives and outcomes that were all dependent on the lens of the protagonist.

I continued to ponder and hypothesise with these observations in both my personal life and at work, where they provided a base for my own reflections and respectful curiosity. It wasn't until some years later, when I serendipitously found myself in the stunning Renaissance city of Florence in the presence of none other than His Holiness the Dalai Lama, that these ideas would begin to take a physical form. While re-reading the notes I had taken on that day, I noticed a diagram that I drew to illustrate what

Introduction

the Dalai Lama had expressed. Essentially, he was sharing the need for a coming together on a global scale. An approach that encouraged groups of people to work together, as opposed to a series of individuals working independently of the other. A more collaborative community. While he acknowledged the importance of peace in order to achieve this approach—to have peace at all levels, both the individual and the group level—it was his emphasis on community and the example he used that caught my attention. The example he used was the European Union. A union that, at the turn of the century, would have been considered a whimsical fantasy, yet today it is reality. I had captured this in my notes as a series of words and dashes that set my mind on fire, and I quickly turned them into a scale of opposites.

From there on, I saw life through a series of opposites, each providing us with a choice. Do we go left, or do we go right? It wasn't long before this idea multiplied into a series of several scales. The merging of my work and studies led to two distinct scales that would represent the tendencies that I noticed and the supporting brain science:

1. Are we focusing on What's Wrong or What's Strong?
2. Are we in safe or unsafe mode?

All the other scales circulating in my head fell neatly beneath these two.

The pages beyond serve to firstly explore and explain the observations, hypotheses, and evidence that went on to form the scales of self-reflection. Then, secondly, they propose a collection of scales as a guide to self-reflection and offer some troubleshooting hints and practical ways to use the scales. You will find reflection tasks scattered throughout the chapters to put into practice the proposed concepts in your own words, experience, and in your own time.

Acknowledgement

In writing this book, I drew on the general observations and themes I noticed while working as a mediator for the Family Court with separating parents. I feel honoured and privileged to have been a part of their lives and uphold complete respect and confidentiality for their journeys.

For this, I thank my many clients who openly and without hesitation let me into their world at times of challenge and change.

To those wonderful souls around me who contributed to the insights I share in this book, I have only praise and gratitude for you. My trusting clients, family, friends, and those who challenged me. Through you, I learnt to see and feel what it meant to lean towards What's Strong—and how it feels when I don't.

CHAPTER 1
THE LACKING

Have you ever felt as though a mass of thick grey clouds was looming directly above you, and only you, following you everywhere you went, only to climax in a crescendo of thunder and lightning that eerily lights up the sky in preparation for the downpour? The kind of storm that has the authorities, radio, and news broadcasters send out a wave of high alerts throughout the city, along with a call for caution and calm. That kind of storm? Yet, strangely, the stormy weather reaches only you, while everyone else seems to be sun-kissed and umbrella-free. It's the kind of storm that not only makes you dash for protective armour but keeps you closed inside where it feels safe and dry.

These kinds of localised, only-for-me thunderstorms of my life prompted me to seek answers about what I observed in myself and those around me. There seemed to be extreme diversity in how people managed their challenges. Methods varied significantly—outcomes did, too. Yet everyone's chosen, or rather inbuilt, challenge management system had deep, complex origins that weren't always obvious.

As a mediator for the Family Court, and in my personal experience, I observed both common threads and remarkable differences. Behind the closed doors of the mediation room, I witnessed similar circumstances play out with surprisingly different outcomes. Expressions of emotion, often instigated by reminders of past events, a disconnect around the current situation, or perhaps uncertainty around a future resolution. The exact details and circumstances varied as much as the results did. Yet, in my observations, the specifics were not as significant as the tendencies that were appearing. What led to anger and frustration and blocked negotiations in one room could result in a mixture of frustration and release, followed by reflection or even agreement, in another room. These observations spurred my curiosity and sent me into reflection mode.

I turned to real-life examples of people who had experienced extreme hardship, people who had not only overcome adversity but had succeeded despite the obstacles. There were stories of inspiration from a diverse range of people, including household names and seemingly ordinary people, yet their outcomes were extraordinary. One that comes to mind was highlighted to me following the release of the movie 'Rocketman' (2019)[1]. This movie did two things—it showed me:
1. how much I love Elton John's music,
2. what it means to be a survivor.

It was like watching Elton reach a point of no return at the hands of unresolved parental conflict and addictions to unhealthy substances, relationships, and behaviour, at a time when society was far less accepting and inclusive.

In the physical world, you could say that the point of change for Elton was going into rehab, yet not everyone who goes into rehab overcomes their addiction. So it was more than a physical change.

While Elton had become my new hero, I had, for some time, preached about Oprah Winfrey as the embodiment of resilience, despite her humble and challenging beginnings. She was the example I never got tired of sharing. I saw her as a woman with direction and a commitment to making a difference.

Her achievements are more than impressive, yet her childhood experience was littered with hardship, betrayal, and pain, including child sexual abuse. I couldn't help but look at her with total and utter admiration and respect. She did not let adversity define or limit her.

The Lacking

As a woman, I felt drawn to, and proud of her. Yet I knew that many other people in this world, perhaps not as famous as Oprah, had similar stories.

There were others whose stories jumped out to me as people who not only overcame their hurdles, but they also did so with tenacity and consistent discipline.

Take Albert Einstein, a man whose name is synonymous with genius. While he was known for the theory of relativity and the famous equation $E=mc^2$, after learning of his early struggles, I came to see him as a man whose energy and resilience kept him on track despite several knock-backs and lack of confidence others showed in him. Others didn't believe in him—but he sure did.

The final example I will share, Turia Pitt, the embodiment of discipline, courage, and determination. At age twenty-four, she suffered severe burns to 65% of her body after getting caught in a grassfire while competing in an ultramarathon. For more than two years, she persisted through over 200 operations, rehabilitation, and relearning basic day-to-day tasks, like walking, to become an inspirational mentor, speaker, writer, and mother. Turia funnelled her physical and emotional pain into recovery and is now devoted to sharing her knowledge and insight with others. A truly remarkable feat in my eyes.

Here were people whose experiences gave them reasons to cry out, to be angry, to look for blame, or even to give up and let the thunderstorm crash down from above. But they did not let a bit of rain dampen their spirit and stop them from moving forward. When I look at these examples, I see a strong sense of self-worth—they believed in themselves with a faith that continually looked forward to what could be, instead of what wasn't.

> **REFLECTION TASK ONE**
>
> 1. Is there anyone you know or know of who has triumphed in the face of adversity?
> 2. What do you admire most about their story? What qualities did they show?
> 3. Choose one quality that you could use to help overcome adversity.

I knew there were lots more stories just like these, scattered through suburbs and neighbourhoods across the world; unnamed and unknown triumphs existed everywhere. Some of these stories belonged to my family and friends who I'd admired and been inspired by, others simply people I'd heard about or crossed paths with whose stories made me sit up and listen with awe. Whether their stories were known or remained untold, they all had or developed a strong sense of self that included:

acceptance of challenges

complete forgiveness

a strong focus on the future

consistent discipline

Not only did the survivors of adversity lean towards these elements, but they did so in a multidimensional way, bringing them to life in every aspect of their being—their thoughts, feelings, and actions—while focusing on What's Strong and dimming out What's Wrong.

For all those who embraced and overcame adversity, with a focus on the future, there existed the opposite. Those who were overcome by their challenges and tendency to hold onto the past. What could these stories teach us?

If those who triumphed, I thought, had a strong sense of self, would that then mean that those who were overcome by their adversity expressed the opposite?

Their sense of self was weakened or not as pronounced, and their focus was What's Wrong while dimming out What's Strong.

They were in a constant state of deficit, a deficit of self I called the 'Lacking'.

> **The Lacking—any thought, feeling, or action that directly or indirectly minimised, doubted, eliminated, or depleted a person's worth or the value of their thoughts, feelings, or actions.**

This Lacking lived and breathed, fuelled by self-doubt and fear. It did not discriminate and often went undercover, hiding silently behind a repertoire of actions that took many forms. It had a way of zooming right in on the individual, cropping out the bigger picture and background. It focused on:

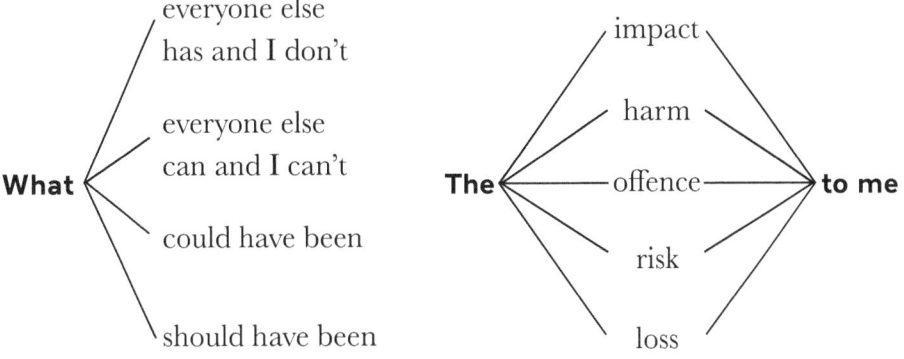

It put this zoomed-in point of view under a microscope and could turn a completely sane and rational person into one with a distorted and narrow view of reality. One where the Self experiences a deficit, while everyone else—the Other—stands to gain.

I found that the Lacking had a melody to it, regardless of whether it was verbalised or remained confined to self-talk, and could sound like:
Why me?
If only he hadn't…?
How could she?
This always happens to me.
No one else cares or understands.
They don't like me.
I didn't get chosen… because I'm not…
I shouldn't have…
I can't…

This Lacking could often accompany matching self-talk. Thoughts riddled with sentiments like shame, criticism, disappointment, and blame.

In its physical form, the embodiment of the Lacking was diverse and mixed. It was not always obvious, making it cunningly deceptive.

What guided the Lacking varied greatly from person to person and could change at any time. There often seemed to be a battle raging between the mind, shown by thoughts, and the body, shown by actions and feelings.

I noticed characteristics or tendencies that emerged as ways to view that world, lenses that demonstrated the essence of the Lacking in action. This included these lenses:
Insecurity
Criticism
Victim mode
Judgement
Denial
Focusing on the past.

When I look at the characteristics of the Lacking with my therapist's hat on, they resemble parts of the stages of grief and loss, a roller-coaster-type wave of emotions that eventually leads to acceptance.

The model above, adapted from the Kübler-Ross model of grief and loss[2], helps us understand, identify, and normalise the feelings that arise because of a loss. The model shows us that it's okay to bounce from one stage to another and then back again before arriving at acceptance, and to normalise the 'I thought I was over this' dread that can often come up when we realise that we are back where we started despite making progress. I saw this in my work a lot. A client would receive an email from the other party, or there would be a decision to make, or there would be some other incident, and it would take them back to anger.

Yet the Lacking isn't necessarily transitional in the way the grief and loss model is designed to give meaning to responses to loss—the Lacking was a lens through which to view the world.

If we see the Lacking as a deficit of self, then the loss that is experienced is internal—an inner loss.

    A loss of self, while not as identifiable as a breakup or death, could be as limiting and live longer than any event or situation. I say a 'loss of self' as the Lacking showed a tendency to view the Self from the 'What's Wrong' stance and it isn't always easily defined.

I noticed that there were valuable lessons to be learnt from not only what is currently happening, but also from what is not happening—namely, the opposite of what is happening. If I am doing X, then I am not doing the opposite of X.

Yet if we see ourselves through a deficit, then the implication is that we are seeing everyone else, the Other, as having greater value than ourselves, regardless of whether this is ever said.

A basic example of this is when we turn to family or friends for their opinion on what we should or shouldn't do. For if I look to another for their opinion, do I not value my own opinion? Or do I see the opinion of others as better in some way than my own? It's very subtle and not always a definite formula, yet I found value in thinking about the potential lessons from what we are not doing. We all ask others for their opinion, yet it doesn't always mean that we have low self-worth or that it is a bad thing.

Let's step aside for a minute back to the trends in handling adversity. Two options had emerged: a lens that focused on 'What's Wrong' or one that focused on 'What's Strong'.

A positive and a negative. This makes the deficient of self or Lacking lens the What's Wrong lens. These two options, opposites, I call a duality; duality number one is related to options that could define all our thoughts, feelings, actions, and beliefs and potentially determine whether we overcome or become consumed by personal crises and challenges.

The Lacking

> **REFLECTION TASK TWO**
>
> Think about how you handle day-to-day stress. Choose a situation you found stressful or challenging—big or small.
> Here are a few examples that you may have experienced:
> *being stuck in traffic*
> *waiting for a friend who is always late*
> *being unable to find your keys or phone*
> *clashing with someone at work*
> *somebody jumping a queue.*
>
> 1. List all the thoughts, feelings, and actions that come up for you around this situation.
> 2. On a blank page, draw two columns, one column with the heading 'What's Wrong' and the other with the heading 'What's Strong'.
> 3. Re-write your list, placing each word in the most appropriate column.
> 4. What do you notice about your columns?

So, there are two options—What's Wrong or What's Strong—to guide our stance. The examples of those who overcame adversity show how a stance materialises into reality. The conclusion is that the direction of our thoughts has the power to enact physical change and should be viewed and treated as real and tangible.

Just look at Elton, as we can see the dramatic turnaround in his life when he decided to do things differently. A reframe, I suspected. We can only go by the physical evidence, the changes, or Elton's actions and speculate that the associated thoughts and feelings also shifted similarly for him.

If our thoughts and emotions are just as powerful as our actions, then the placebo effect makes perfect sense. What I mean by placebo effect is when people get better because they think they are taking medication designed to heal their condition. This is considered in more detail in The Evidence, Chapter 3 of this book.

I thought of myself as a positive person, yet in reality I carried disappointments and had adopted a 'needs improvement' approach to many parts of me. This was the belief that things will be better when..., yet the 'when' was generally an external event, something that would come to me and completely change my life. Something that would generally take place in the future, and that, for whatever reason, was currently out of reach for me.

The home truth was that positivity wasn't always my default position, and I routinely unconsciously leaned into What's Wrong, all the while thinking and believing that I was full speed ahead towards What's Strong.

If we look back at the elements of the sense of self in those who triumphed, we will notice that they would all appear under the What's Strong column:

acceptance

forgiveness

future focus

discipline

They were more than just positive thoughts; they were multidimensional ways of being that could be transposed into actions and emotions that filled their daily lives. An approach that seeped into all aspects of what it means to be human. They lived it in day-to-day life in a way that was undecidedly leaning towards strength, the opposite of the Lacking.

The discipline component required physical action, something you can see, and it would be matched with corresponding thoughts and beliefs.

Anyone who has ever tried to lose weight might understand that discipline is not just physical, and how long you can hold a plank is often more dependent on the strength of your mind—your internal coach who pushes and cheers you through the plank—than your physical strength. It requires a multidimensional approach.

The next two elements—acceptance and forgiveness—again called for, interestingly enough, a multidimensional approach, and they relied on each other before moving towards a future focus.

Staying with the weight loss example, I have a fantastic workout plan, join a gym, start walking, and watch what I eat. My plan starts well, yet for some reason, it dwindles before I get a chance to see solid results. I get bored of walking, feel uncomfortable at the gym, or my training partner is no longer available when I am. I have placed some conditions on my actions:

I will only walk if it's not boring.
I will only go to the gym if I have the latest gym clothes.
I will not go unless my training partner is there.

These conditions inevitability make my desired outcome more challenging or delayed. Have I accepted the situation?

When I am met with resistance that may appear as a reasonably logical justification for not sticking to my plan and generally highlights What's Wrong, this is a clue that some aspect of acceptance is diminished. This diminished acceptance might result in self-criticism. I beat myself up for not reaching my targets, which leads me to feel ashamed and disappointed with myself; I am anything but forgiving.

The big take-home message for me wasn't just about the power and need for positive thought that pointed towards a What's Strong lens. The What's Strong lens had to be embodied in all aspects of the lived experience. Living it meant:

Think it—*as shown by the quality of my thoughts, beliefs, self-talk, and reflection.*

Feel it—*as shown by the associated emotions (Do I feel good or bad?).*

Show it—*as shown by actions, what is physically being done or not done.*

It just took one of these to be missing or leaning towards What's Wrong to undo everything, and no one would ever know. The evidence—what was happening—would point to a deficiency somewhere along the line in the 'live it' chain. One of which was consciously or unconsciously leaning towards What's Wrong.

REFLECTION TASK THREE

Now go back to your example of a stressful or challenging situation from page 19.

1. What would you be thinking in that situation if your response stemmed from the What's Strong lens?

2. What emotions might you be feeling in that situation if your response stemmed from the What's Strong lens?

3. What would you be doing in that situation if your response stemmed from the What's Strong lens?

So how do we know if we are living the What's Strong lens if it wasn't always obvious?

A mirror—that's what would help determine if we are really living it. A glance into a mirror, with a willingness to stay there long enough without judgment to accept and understand the reflection: self-reflection.

Before I could truly live it, I had to face it without judgement. A consequence of this would be an opportunity for personal growth and lessons that would guide future experiences and challenges.

Perhaps my work and training had made me more sensitive to the notion of maintaining a non-judgemental stance. It was a fundamental part of being a mediator, being the independent third party, and is what differentiated my work from the traditional legal system. This non-judgemental stance that my role demanded also built an awareness of words that would see me form internal guidelines around what to say or not say. I found that this non-judgemental approach encouraged open and respectful communication, allowing some difficult conversations to take place.

REFLECTION TASK FOUR

1. Think of a time you had a conversation with someone where you felt completely accepted and respected.
    a. Write three words to describe their approach or what they did or said. For example, they may have:
    acknowledged
    encouraged
    supported
    forgiven
    shown compassion.
    b. Which column would these words sit under: What's Wrong or What's Strong?

2. Think of a time when you had a conversation with someone where you felt judged and disrespected.
    a. Write three words to describe their approach or what they did or said. For example, they may have:
    criticised
    blamed
    discouraged
    judged
    minimised
    been unsympathetic.
    b. Which column would these words sit under: What's Wrong or What's Strong?

3. Complete this sentence to act as a guide to your non-judgemental self-reflection and self-talk.

    I listen with   **and respond with**

The Lacking

The characteristics of the Lacking were words of judgement that leaned towards What's Wrong. If we apply the idea that there are valuable learnings to be had when we explore opposites (what's not happening), the opposite of the Lacking would then logically look to words of non-judgement that leaned towards What's Strong.

CHAPTER 2

THE STRENGTH

When I thought of polarities, I was taken back to earlier in my career. One which had commenced with an 'I better take what I am given' approach because I'm not as experienced as everyone else. Try as I might to shake this off, it had become part of my narrative. So, when I began working as a family mediator with an organisation that prided itself on its 'strengths-based' approach, I was completely taken off guard and left with the same sense of satisfaction and pride that a toddler who recently discovered how to walk backwards would show.

I was getting paid to do something I enjoyed and was in an environment where those around me were consistently providing evidence of how well I was working. This philosophy steered towards vision and hope by drawing on existing strengths, interests, and support. It was an approach that was to become instilled in my practice.

It was an empowering approach that sought to enable an individual to control and direct the process of change[3]. As opposed to placing focus on the problem or issue at hand, which, by its nature, was more likely to point to a deficit or what lacked. While it was generally in my nature to see the good in others, my learnt default mode saw me struggling to see the good in myself. It was also one of the first times in my working life that I truly felt valued and appreciated. My ideas about processes and day-to-day work were encouraged, even applauded. My manager would routinely offer me opportunities or cases that showcased and supported my abilities. My opinions and ideas were not only considered but routinely appreciated and endorsed.

For me, it was a thoughtful approach, one that was perfectly catered to me. A side effect, I found, was that I also began to believe more in myself, and my actions showed it. I could see and feel the benefits of this approach and found that the more exposure I had to it, the more I used it in my practice.

It was as though the volume of my self-worth and appreciation had gone up a notch as the focus shifted to my strengths. In doing so, it embraced, applauded, and respected my individuality and self-determination. It looked at What's Strong rather than What's Wrong.

We live in a world where we are routinely exposed to, and by default focus on, What's Wrong. So the switch to What's Strong can feel unnatural and perhaps even forced or unrealistic. We go to a doctor when we have symptoms, and we expect that the doctor will identify the cause and propose a treatment. Their patients have placed trust and faith in them to find a solution.

I also noticed this in both my work and my personal life—problems presented in search of a solution, generally at the hands of a third person. Not exactly the hallmarks of a strengths-based approach that looks to empower a self-determined solution.

REFLECTION TASK FIVE

1. Write down one quality that you consider a weakness. For example, 'I take a long time to make decisions.'

2. Rewrite it as a strength by highlighting one good thing about this quality or how this quality has helped you. For example, 'I consider all the available information when I make a decision.'

3. What do you think about this quality when you read the rewrite?

The strengths-based approach often called for a rewrite, which is perhaps why I was drawn to the idea of narrative mediation, which is a process designed to explore and extract an individual's strengths and capacity for self-determination. It provides a way to rewrite or reconstruct the script, one where the protagonist could willingly change roles and go from victim to survivor. It was a strengths-based approach that emphasised the use and impact of language and meaning. It also separated the people from the problem and externalised what was happening in the hope of giving it a new perspective.[4]

This idea was, coincidently, put in the spotlight by William Ury and Roger Fisher's bestselling book 'Getting to Yes'. The first element in the method of negotiation that they propose is – separate the people from the problem. This detachment from the point in question was a way of creating distance and externalising the issue.[5]

So then how can we lean towards What's Strong when we might naturally or instinctively go towards What's Wrong? Fisher & Ury would provide a clue—separate the people from the problem.

This distance gives perspective, another view, which I suspected was part of 'flipping' What's Wrong to What's Strong. A good amount of distance could support and encourage a What's Strong rewrite.

Could being our own mediator, the independent third party who does not judge—could it be that this concept would aid reflection?

Reflection—it could heal and transform and do so with respect.

The risk was that the process ended up camouflaged or overtaken by self-talk and self-criticism, which invariably placed the spotlight on 'What's Wrong', and with a vengeance. This distinction was crucial to me as a confessed over-thinker.

In the Lacking chapter, we saw self-reflection as a non-judgemental conversation with yourself, one that is aimed at providing opportunities for growth and learning. We also concluded that the characteristics of the Lacking lean towards What's Wrong.

The emergence of a strengths-based approach was undecidedly leaning towards What's Strong, the very opposite of the Lacking. If we flipped the Lacking, it would convert to the Strength:

> **insecure** *flipped to* **secure.**
> **criticism** *flipped to* **respect.**
> **victim** *flipped to* **survivor.**
> **judgement** *flipped to* **understanding.**
> **past focus** *flipped to* **future focus.**

This flip moved away from What's Wrong to What's Strong, and it did so with a wide-angle lens that extended to the needs of the collective. The Lacking focused solely on the 'me'—what happened to me, what was done to me, how it impacted me, what I have to do—while the Strength added a global aspect that encompassed both the Self and Others and said, 'I see What's Strong in and towards myself and I see What's Strong in and towards others.'

The Strength, like its opposite, was multidimensional. It could manifest in words, thoughts, feelings, beliefs, actions, or inaction:

what I think, say, and believe
what I feel
what I show or do.

It was a reframing of the Lacking, often resembling a positive affirmation and could sound like:

I've learnt from this.
There will be another opportunity.
I did the best I could.
It was my choice.
We just didn't work out.
I won't let this stop me.
She did the best she could.

It was, without question, much easier for me to come up with examples of the Lacking. They flowed more naturally, which is perhaps an indication that the Lacking was my default position and examples were readily available and in my mind. The reframe towards the Strength, I realised, wasn't always second nature.

I'd come across many people who leaned towards the Lacking and those who leaned towards the Strength, and I'd seen many versions of both in the actions of myself and others.

We know there are two options: What's Wrong and What's Strong. The Lacking or the Strength. It seemed easy enough to understand—opposites. In the examples of those who triumphed in the face of adversity, we saw the importance and value of the What's Strong path as the big difference between overcoming or being overcome.

We live in a world where there may be reasons to jump between the lens, back and forth between What's Wrong and What's Strong. One lens might prove more dominant at certain times; what's more important is the ability to identify when What's Wrong had kicked in, reflect without judgement, and take on the learnings. It isn't so much about what we are doing or have done. It was about what we can learn from it and how long it takes us to extract that knowledge from within ourselves. With absolutely no care or importance on the lessons or the time frame of anybody else. Just the self. Like any skill, the more we practise, the more natural that skill begins to feel. Practice is the best master.

The flip towards What's Strong called for a rewrite guided by healthy self-reflection, something which I visualised using the following equation:

What's Strong = self-reflection + rewriting towards the strength

This equation reminded me of ideas discussed at a self-love workshop I attended. One line that stood out for me and stayed both in my memory and the notes I took on that day was:

'Be the compassionate friend to self.'

I cross-referenced this with notes I had taken at a conference on compassion.[6] One of the keynote speakers, Professor Stephen Porges, a man who eloquently blended neuroscience and compassion, described compassion from the point of view of the therapist as 'the ability to witness other people's feelings, respect and acknowledge them without being hurt by the expression of the other's feelings' (paraphrased from the notes I took).

What attracted my attention was the notion of compassion as the ability to witness with respect something that supported and encouraged a strengths-based view, while also providing some detachment.

It had been some time since I sat in a lecture on the rules of evidence, yet somehow the ideas were still somewhere in the back of my mind. The role of the witness was quite specific and limited to details of what they saw. Anything outside this could not be submitted as evidence. A witness does not give their opinion, assumptions, theory, or interpretation.[7] For example:

Example 1: *I saw Anthony and Francis walking across the road at 11.33 a.m. on 5th May.*

Example 2: *I saw Anthony and Francis walking across the road at 11.33 a.m. on 5th May. I think they were going to the pub down the road because I have seen them there in the past.*

While example 2 might make an interesting conversation piece, it cannot be relied upon in court. It's inadmissible.

> **REFLECTION TASK SIX**
>
> 1. Describe, in your own words, the role of a witness.
> 2. Now consider the opposite. What is it that a witness does not do?

If self-reflection is a non-judgemental conversation with yourself, then it seemed only natural to merge this concept with those expressed by Professor Stephen Porges—to witness with respect.

When we refer back to the Lacking and the Strength, we see that the flipside of judgement is understanding. So now, a non-judgemental conversation becomes a conversation that shows understanding.

When applying the same flip to respect in reverse, we get criticism. Remember, there are valuable learnings from both what is happening and what is not happening. Respect means to be free of criticism. So, to witness with respect is essentially to witness (without judgement/to show understanding) with respect (free from criticism).

My work made me aware of language and the impact that it could have on a respectful and open conversation. As a mediator, a non-judgemental stance was demanded, yet its importance was really only highlighted when it was perceived as missing or questioned. For in those cases, conversations would shut down and become almost impossible.

When I am personally confronted with judgmental language or questions that focus on What's Wrong, I go into a defence mode that will see me either shut down or attack.

If judgement could easily close down conversations, a judgement-free approach could open up and allow difficult conversations to take place.

At this point, you might like to review your responses to Reflection Task Four as you begin to consider how you can have a non-judgemental conversation with yourself.

While Professor Stephen Porges was talking about being compassionate towards others, why couldn't we use these same principles towards ourselves, showing compassion to ourselves?

REFLECTION TASK SEVEN

1. Think about what makes someone a compassionate person.

2. Make a list of some of the qualities that you associate with a compassionate person.

3. Choose one of these qualities and write down what a compassionate person might do or say as an expression of that quality?

4. Reflect on your answers above and write down one way you can show compassion to yourself.

It only seems natural that compassion be added to the equation, which now reads as: Flip towards What's Strong = self-reflection + rewrite towards the Strength + compassion. While it made sense, the equation still seemed a little unbalanced. Was it that the flip towards Strength and the rewrite towards What's Strong was the same thing?

That would make the new equation:

What's Strong = self-reflection + compassion

That sounded decidedly better and cemented in my mind the formula for an approach that would support and encourage a flip towards What's Strong, one which included compassionate self-reflection as key.

When I re-observed the tendencies in managing personal crises—our inbuilt challenge-management system—I saw that approaches could differ not only from person to person but also from situation to situation. It was what initially led me to seek out examples of those who overcame adversity. I thought that the stages of grief and loss also played a part here, as mediations that took place closer to the point of separation or after an incident often moved slower. Yet it did not mean that people were not capable of coming together in good faith soon after separating or after an incident.

It was more about how the individual operated than the passing of time. If the passing of time was the only factor, I would be less likely to have return clients. It was the lens applied at any given point in time: a Lacking lens or a strength lens, which would be used to view:

the self
others.

A lens that could determine where and who the spotlight is placed on, for wherever the light shone, it would naturally leave the surroundings—people, places, or situations—in a dim light. Is the spotlight on What's Wrong or What's Strong?

My work with and observations of our inbuilt challenge management system, along with the seemingly inescapable wave of emerging brain science, would be to add another layer of evidence in support of the strengths-based approach.

Could history and science hold clues as to why some naturally lean towards What's Wrong while others lean towards What's Strong?

CHAPTER 3

THE EVIDENCE

Once upon a time, life on planet Earth was completely offline and our ancestors roamed the lands we walk on today. The nine-to-five routine we live by had no place in that world. Instead, communities lived off the land in small numbers for self-protection and survival.

As our surroundings and habits continued to develop, so did we, adding layers of adjustments and extras to the structure of our brains. Additions to our more primitive versions. While the challenges our ancestors faced differed greatly from those of today, biologically, we share the same hardware.[8]

Our brain was like a renovated old home—the foundations remained the same, supporting additions, updates, and new technology alongside original features. All working together as one seamless structure.

Those original features included the ancient part of our brain that is driven by impulse and threat-detection. Always on the lookout for danger and acting on instinct. It was a miraculously efficient data-collecting machine.

Our renovated brain had a team of security guards on call 24/7 scanning for potential danger and ready to go into protection mode at the slightest hint of harm. When they sound the alarm, all the attention is on them and what they need your body to do. Launching focus towards basic automatic functions aimed at bringing you back to safety. Consequently, there is limited energy going into anything else, like any form of strengths-based self-reflection.

Yet this team of security guards is acting in anticipation of threat or danger—it's predicting threat as opposed to reacting to threat.

It is drawing on past stored experience and knowledge of danger just in case it turns out to be danger this time.[9]

Have you ever felt something on your arm and automatically started rigorously jolting your arm around, expecting to see a hideous spider or something equally as repulsive, only to realise that a leaf had drifted down and gently brushed the side of your arm? A pre-emptive strike—just in case it was something horrid.

Today, our day-to-day, non-life-threatening stresses activate the same survival mode our ancestors had relied upon in life-threatening situations, using prediction to anticipate and act on threats.

This notion took me back to a book I read in high school 'Lord of the Flies', by the Nobel Prize-winning author William Golding. It's the story of a group of well-educated children who find themselves stranded on a deserted island and face the challenges of day-to-day survival, including attempts to govern themselves. Without giving away too much to those of you who haven't read the book or watched the movie, what we see is almost a reverse evolution as the group begins to revert to more primitive ways. Survival mode becomes the default in the small community threatened by division and driven by fear.[10]

Yet why was it that, as a species, our responses to threats, challenges, and stress varied dramatically?

It wasn't just our ancient, built-in survival instincts that contributed to how we manage a personal crisis. There was also negative bias. A double whammy—not only are we biologically designed to be paranoid, but we are also negative. Negative bias meant that we would remember, recognise, and react more strongly to negative stimuli. So we would effectively give more weight to an insult (What's Wrong) over any praise (What's Strong) of equal value. In the same way, a traumatic experience is recalled before a positive one. Essentially, we are wired to highlight or focus on What's Wrong.[11]

> **REFLECTION TASK EIGHT**
>
> 1. Think about this common question: How are you?
> 2. For the next week, notice the response you and others provide to this question.
> 3. Notice whether the responses are leaning towards What's Wrong or What's Strong.
> 4. Were there any responses that you remember more than others?

I could see that the origins of the Lacking were, in fact, pointing towards the origins of humanity and the instinctive mechanisms that kick in when a threat is anticipated. In the most eloquent summary of Charles Darwin's Origin of Species, and what would have to be one of the most misattributed Darwin quotes, a Professor of Management and Marketing at Louisiana State University, Leon C Megginson, stated: 'According to Darwin's Origin of Species, it is not the most intellectual of the species that survives; it is not the strongest of the species that survives, but the species that survives is the one that is best able to adapt to and adjust to the changing environment in which it finds itself.'[12]

This really went hand in hand with Professor Stephen Porges' reframing of behaviour as adaptations to one's experience. The idea that what we think, feel, and do is a reflection of our surroundings.[13]

As our evolution continued, we became a species that belonged to groups—families within communities—and our brains had no choice but to change and grow in order to manage our relationships. Basic life functions and impulses were not enough.[14]

> **'No man is an island.'**
> —John Donne[15]

The thirteenth-century Holy Roman Emperor Fredrick II was a man who, by all accounts, had a passion for science and was known for often conducting rather cruel experiments, including a language deprivation experiment. He wished to ascertain if there was one natural language of mankind, a language that would ultimately, he thought, be the language of God. He ordered a group of babies to be raised free from any interaction that wasn't absolutely necessary. They were raised by nurses whose job was simply to feed and bathe them. The emperor was hoping that they would grow up free from outside influence and eventually speak the language they were born with. Tragically, they all died.[16]

This sadly reminded me of the Romanian orphans whose images shocked the world in 1990 and became the subject of research on the impact of social deprivation and neglect in early life. Years after many of these children were adopted, social and emotional issues were found to be commonplace.[17]

Turning to the 'still face' experiments carried out by the brilliant developmental psychologist Ed Tronick, his work showed the profound developmental impact of the quality of mother-infant interaction at a time when it was thought that infants could not engage in social interaction.

Even though I've viewed the clips on YouTube many times, I still find them a little difficult to watch. They start with typical mother/baby interaction, baby talk, eye contact, and playing together until the mother suddenly stops and becomes expressionless and non-responsive. In a crescendo of smiles, babbles, hand gestures, and sounds, you see the baby's response gradually transition from joy to anguish that increases as the baby desperately reaches out for engagement.[18]

When we consider this research alongside the experiments of Emperor Fredrick II and the Romanian orphans, the common element that stands out is the lack of meaningful communication or interactions.

It wasn't just about relationships but the quality of relationships that mattered, and it would be a longitudinal study spanning over eighty years that demonstrated the effect of this. The study was conducted at Harvard University, commencing in 1938 during the Great Depression, and was aimed at tracing the physical and emotional health of participants over their lifetime in an attempt to discover insights into healthy ageing. George E Vaillant, principal investigator of the study, concluded that 'warmth of relationships' was the biggest factor influencing life satisfaction, and quite simply, 'Happiness is love. Full stop'.[19]

Again, the quality of the surrounding relationships was a key indicator, which goes hand in hand with Charles Darwin's work and Professor Stephen Porges' notion that we are adaptations to our experience.

Interaction is not only the fuel for our growing brains; it also sets the foundations and the default positions stored in the biological memories that we later draw on, helping us to efficiently predict and respond to future situations and events.[20] These are the factors that contribute to whether we lean towards What's Wrong or What's Strong.

The importance and influence of the early stages of life—the first one thousand days, in particular—has been the subject of many studies around the world and is a commonly accepted concept of child development. It is the quality of the interactions, care, and environment during the first one thousand days of life—from conception—that lay the foundations for the adult that the babbling baby will become. The nature of the first one thousand days could predict adult outcomes. It's a time when a baby is collecting data to determine what it needs to survive in its surroundings as it looks to its carer for cues of safety, in tune with the work of Ed Tronick. These were cues like connection, touch, eye contact, language—essentially anything that would reduce stress and promise safety.[21]

The experience begins to guide the development of an infant's brain with adaptations to match it. This approach taught me to view behaviour as an adaptation to change, as opposed to labelling it as a behavioural issue or problem. At the same time, these adaptations provide clues on the quality of one's past experience.

I saw this a lot in my work with parents who raised concerns about their children's behaviour. They served to make me curious about the child's experience and what it was that made that child adapt in the way they did.

Our early experience didn't only translate into adaptions; it would also infiltrate our physical wellbeing, and numerous studies have linked specific poor health outcomes with negative childhood experiences.

One in particular was the Adverse Childhood Experiences Study (ACE Study) originally conducted by Kaiser Permanente. Participants were recruited to the study between 1995 and 1997 and asked to complete a questionnaire about their childhood experiences. More specifically, there were ten questions about adverse experiences in three categories: childhood abuse, neglect, and household challenges. The study found multiple links between childhood adversity and health impairments in the adult years and that the greater the number of adverse childhood experiences, the greater the likelihood of health problems later in life.[22]

> **REFLECTION TASK NINE**
>
> 1. Re-read part of this chapter from the section under the quote 'No man is an island' and write down anything you would highlight as points that stood out for you.
>   You may also like to watch the Ed Tronick still face experiment on Youtube
> 2. Why did they stand out for you?
> 3. Reflect on this information in light of your own experience and that of others with whom you come in contact.
>   This can be a confronting task; you should show compassion with yourself during this process, which may mean completing this task at another time. If it feels right, you may consider speaking to someone who can help you with your understanding of this, like a counsellor or psychologist.

My simplistic summary so far is that we are beings who perceive, process, and act on our surroundings in search of safety, yet what is safe differs greatly. At times, safety means running away from, avoiding, or seeking reassurance, while at other times it means going towards, leaping in, stepping forward. Our built-in memory helps us predict what to go towards and what to move away from. What and how we remember is also heavily impacted by the quality of our early relationships and interactions, something that could also have ramifications for our adult physical wellbeing.

I see memory as a collection of the internal stories that forge the basis for how we respond to certain situations. A rewrite of these memories would require more mental effort and energy than simply sticking with the default carved by our experience. That's why change is hard; it's re-writing the default memories.

On top of this, our instincts have naturally evolved to be more sensitive to fear and pain than to pleasure and reward.[23] This meant that between the Lacking and Strength, the Lacking could have more pull because it invokes feelings of fear and pain. Another factor that gave pain more weight was the science that had shown that our brains treat physical pain and social pain in a very similar way and that the same can be said for physical and social pleasure.

Pain was pain; with or without bruising, it could leave scars.

Social pain was almost akin to physical pain from the brain's perspective and included things like:

social exclusion
mourning or loss
being treated unfairly
painful emotions from comparing oneself to others
envy.

Conversely, being socially accepted, having a good reputation, receiving cooperation, being treated fairly, as well as schadenfreude—the pleasure derived from the misfortune of others and the opposite of envy—are akin to social rewards or pleasure, which the brain registers in a way that is very similar to physical pleasure or reward.[24]

The Evidence

> **REFLECTION TASK TEN**
>
> 1. Review your common cause of day-to-day stress from Reflection Task Two on page 19.
> 2. Does it fall within the list of social pain above?
> 3. If so, what is the impact of social pain on your day-to-day stress?

What surprised me the most was that negative social comparisons caused social pain. It gave a deeper, painful meaning to 'the grass is always greener on the other side', particularly when we live in a society filled with advertisements, social media and marketing that can serve to highlight comparisons through the Lacking lens or what is missing in comparison with another. These kinds of comparisons could invoke real pain.

Some representations of social pain resemble characteristics of the Lacking, which only further added to the power, impact, and influence of our thoughts.

Thoughts can make us feel pain.

From the brain's perspective, feeling judged or treated unfairly was extremely similar to the experience of physical pain and only emphasised the value of non-judgemental self-reflection. What's Wrong mode could feel like physical pain.

This served as a warning for all overthinkers or anyone who ever spent time on catastrophic hypothesis, internal analysis, going over the worst-case scenario 'What ifs' and negative self-talk—for it had the potential to result in self-induced pain. They all focused on what was 'wrong' and further heightened the value and necessity of flipping it to what was 'strong'.

> **REFLECTION TASK ELEVEN**
>
> 1. Think of a time that you felt judged, excluded, treated unfairly, or rejected. It may have been in a social setting, a break-up, a nasty comment, or being cut off or left out.
>
> 2. On a scale of one to ten, where one is no pain and ten is severe pain, rate the social pain that you experienced.
>
> 3. How did you feel about the person or situation in question?
>
> 4. Now think of a time that your analysis of a situation or self-talk negatively judged your thoughts, feelings, or actions.
>
> 5. On a scale of one to ten, where one is no pain and ten is severe pain, rate the social pain you experienced.
>
> 6. How do you feel about yourself during this time?
>
> 7. What would your self-analysis sound like if it viewed the situation through the Strength lens?

Survival ensured that we were naturally more sensitive to fear and pain than to pleasure and reward and that the memories of our experience would shape how we responded to life in the day-to-day. This is how our default lenses formed, but it doesn't mean they can't shift. Our brains can change. This is a concept that Norman Doidge introduced to me.

He spoke about possibilities, hope, and healing in his book The Brain That Changes Itself. The title was a succinct statement about neuroplasticity, the discovery that the brain can physically change through mental experience or learning.

This is internal structural change due to internal factors—mental experience.[25]

His book referred to the work of Alvaro Pascual-Leone, whose study showed that thoughts could physically change brain structure. He was able to do this with the help of two groups of people, both of which had never played the piano. One group was to practise playing the notes they were taught while the other was to visualise practising the same notes. Each group practised the same piece for the same duration of study.

His experiments revealed that doing something, or thinking about doing something, produced very similar and even some identical physical changes in the brain.[26]

REFLECTION TASK TWELVE

1. Write down a repetitive thought or worry that you have had lately. For example, *'I am not happy at work.'*

2. Now write down a statement that is the opposite of that worry. For example, *'I am happy at work.'*

3. Ask yourself why the opposite of your worry, your statement, is important to you. For example, *'It's important to me that I am happy at work because this makes me feel satisfied and motivated to do my job.'*

4. Again, ask yourself why your answer to Question 3 is important to you. For example, *'It's important to me that I feel satisfied and motivated to do my job because I take pride in my work.'* What have you learnt from the rewrite of your worry or repetitive thought?

5. Write down three reasons these lessons are important.

Thoughts were indeed powerful, and the brain showed it. Was this the reason behind the placebo effect? 'The Placebo Experiment: Can My Brain Cure My Body?' (2018) was a Michael Mosley documentary where over 100 people participated in the study, all of whom had reported chronic back pain. They were told there was a new super-drug that they were going to test. They were, in fact, all given a pill that contained ground-up rice, yet after the experiments, 45% of the participants reported a medical improvement. The belief was enough to kick the body and brain into healing mode.[27]

The power of our intangible thoughts has tangible impacts. This is a concept that also makes change biologically challenging, requiring continued persistence to go against the default position—positions that were established by our historical adaptations to past experiences, yet they inform our present and future.

REFLECTION TASK THIRTEEN

1. Consider the topics explored in this chapter.
2. Now imagine you have a friend who is a chronic overthinker. List the top three points from this chapter that you would share with them and why you think they are important.

CHAPTER 4
THE EVOLUTION OF THE SCALES

The more I reflected on the evidence, the science, and my observations, the more the complexity of our existence appeared to be in stark contrast to the simplicity of our needs. Safety, above all, was paramount, yet for every situation, the level of safety we felt could determine which path we chose. The result was that there were multiple potential endings for every situation we faced, and these endings corresponded with the level of safety.

An unsafe experience could be registered in our memory and referred to in the future, even becoming our default path. In reality, this could look like whether we had a tendency to lean towards the Lacking or the Strength.

The idea that we can classify our tendencies using opposites is the basis for the scales of self-reflection. Stemming from my visual representation of the comments made by the Dalai Lama, I interpreted and recorded his call for a shift from the 'me' lens to the 'we' lens in my notes in this way:

Individual ▸ *Family* ▸ *Community* ▸ *Global*

My rewrite of this became the first scale, a starting point to plot an experience or situation.

Individual ◄――――► Community

That was how the first scale was born. If we go back to brain science, a set of polarities appears to form the biological point of view.

Unsafe ◄――――► Safe

Our brains are designed to scan for signs of danger and find themselves going instinctively into unsafe mode until there is a return to safety, the biological scale.

In the Lacking chapter, we saw polarities in our thoughts, feelings, and actions. They were either closer to What's Wrong or closer to What's Strong—another fundamental scale.

What's Wrong ◄――――► What's Strong

In bringing together the characteristics of the Lacking and the characteristics of the Strength, further scales appear, all of which fall neatly beneath the two above, almost like a ladder.

The Evolution of the Scales

The Lacking is on the left while the Strength is on the right.

The Lacking		The Strength
Unsafe	↔	Safe
What's Wrong	↔	What's Strong
Individual	↔	Community
Insecure	↔	Secure
Criticism	↔	Respect
Victim	↔	Survivor
Judgement	↔	Understanding
Past	↔	Future

They provide an external platform for self-reflection and a reminder of what was not happening in pointing out alternate options. By looking at where the spotlight is facing, we see both where the focus is and where the focus isn't—what is being dimmed out. Duality number one is a polarity, which could plot situations, events, experiences, or responses, past, present, and future.

The scales weren't just about plotting which side you are on; they could also give you a perspective of the other person's experience, as the closer you are to one side, the further away you are from the other. This is where the spotlight served to highlight who it is facing. Duality number two—the characters, the Self and the Other.

For if I (Self) was criticising someone, I was not showing them (Other) respect.

The scales did not stop with the characteristics of the Strength and the Lacking. Others could easily be added. I turned to the examples of those who triumphed in the face of adversity, and the scales expanded to include:

Additional Scales

Blame ⟷ Empowerment

Denial ⟷ Acceptance

Assumption ⟷ Evidence

Punishment ⟷ Forgiveness

These additions made the updated ladder of the scales of self-reflection as follows:

Updated Ladder of the Scales of Self-Reflection

Unsafe ⟷ Safe

What's Wrong ⟷ What's Strong

Individual ⟷ Community

Insecure ⟷ Secure

Criticism ⟷ Respect

Victim ⟷ Survivor

Judgement ⟷ Understanding

Past ⟷ Future

Blame ⟷ Empowerment

Denial ⟷ Acceptance

Assumption ⟷ Evidence

Punishment ⟷ Forgiveness

As my observations merged into a physical tool, I began to refer to them for both my work and personal situations, whether it was about my role as the mediator, analysing my chosen approach, or reflecting on a personal conversation. This tool allowed me to categorise my contribution as What's Wrong or What's Strong. Confronting, at times, yet it was compassionately powerful. For if I was faced with someone who tended to use criticism and blame, the way I witnessed this would say much more about me than anyone else. Did I respond with judgement or with understanding? Something that was born from my observations of how others manage personal crises was proving to be a simple way to transform what would otherwise be my overthinking into self-reflection. It was witnessing with respect.

REFLECTION TASK FOURTEEN

1. Choose a scale that you will observe in yourself for the next week.

2. At the end of the week, reflect on what jumped out for you during your week of observations.

3. Write down a statement about how you will continue to apply your chosen scale. For example, 'I listen with respect' or 'I respond with understanding'.

CHAPTER 5

THE SCALES

I thought it only right to explore each scale in more detail and start with the scale that inspired all the others.

Individual ↔ Community	
On the left, we find the 'me' approach, which sees through a narrow lens and zooms in on me	On the right is the 'we' approach, which sees through a wide-angle lens, including others.

Here is what I might be thinking, saying, or focusing on in the individual stance:

the impact on me
how I can benefit
what I have a right to do
what I need
what I want.

There once was a time when people could smoke on a plane. This is what I think of when I consider this scale. A clear example of an individual's needs in conflict with those of the surrounding group or community. In this case, the 'Other' is the passengers and cabin crew.

While this might be an obvious example, there are day-to-day examples that might not be as pronounced. A clue is what the spotlight is highlighting. Is it zoomed in on one individual? Or does the view include the broader surroundings?

There are, of course, situations where the need for safety prevails and requires the spotlight to zoom in on an individual.

I am exploring situations when safety is not compromised or threatened.

The competing interests might include:

All decisions or considerations revolve around what I need or want and is best for me	**Versus**	the needs and wants of the group as a whole—what is best for the group.
My right to do something or not do something	**Versus**	respecting and acknowledging the impact on and needs of the group and acting accordingly.
A right to do or not do something	**Versus**	the responsibilities that come with the exercising of this right.

This one is tricky because it's not always obvious and not always a bad thing to set boundaries to ensure your own needs are met. It's more about a view of the world that consistently only zooms in on one individual.

In the day-to-day, the Lacking side of this scale might look like an individual proposing an activity or event because it suits their lifestyle and needs even though it might disadvantage or put out some of the others in the group, which may include family, colleagues, acquaintances, or friends. For example, my desire to go to a restaurant that suits my taste and budget versus considering the tastes and budget of the group, family, or friends also attending.

Essentially, this is when an individual's needs conflict with those of the couple, the family, the group, the team, or the community they belong to. This might also present as an individual's right to do or not do something, where not protecting or enforcing that right could result in a potential or perceived loss.

When I'm in the Individual stance, I have a fear of experiencing a personal Lacking unless I take action to protect myself and prevent myself being:

overlooked
undervalued
unsatisfied
exploited

> Insecure ← → Secure
>
> On the left, we have the 'me' approach, emphasising a deficit of self.
>
> On the right is stability, with a generous amount of self-worth.

Here is what I might be thinking, saying, or focusing on in the insecure stance:

Everybody else has it better than me.
I have to show them how wrong they are.
I don't trust my decisions.
How can I be like everyone else?
What is it that I'm missing?
My voice or opinion isn't good enough to be shared.
I'll show them what I know; I am smart and knowledgeable, too.
I won't try.

This is where the dreaded force of comparison arises to fuel and further nurture insecurity. When I compared myself to others and what they were doing, it highlighted what I wasn't doing. Where I was and how I felt that day would determine how much weight I gave it and the resulting impact on me.

Outwardly, comparing could look like a comment that undermines or questions the experience of another. Inwardly, it could feel like the self-berating and continual rumination highlighting what is wrong with yourself.

It could also present as confidence, the 'I am competent and that I need everyone to know it' stance, so I will routinely correct people and speak up to show how much I know. Conversely, it could present as not speaking up, not asking questions or sharing knowledge for fear of being wrong or simply not good or smart enough. When I look at this scale, it's like a see-saw of strengths and weaknesses.

The competing interests might include:

I want people to like me	**Versus**	showing my true essence.
My perception of self	**Versus**	showing my true essence.
What I think they think of me	**Versus**	showing my true essence.

Many actions can fall under this scale, as it's a state of being that may differ slightly from the other scales while also overlapping onto them. It is not something we do—it's what we are or show when we act in a particular way. The actions presented in some of the other scales may be different versions of this one and point back to insecure/secure actions.

I might think, talk, and act in a way that satisfies my need to be right because it makes me feel validated when I am right and you are wrong, adding to my sense of self at the expense of the other. In doing so, I might be critical or judgmental of others and open to only my perspective.

Conversely, if I don't know the answer or solution, I might fall into the pattern of seeking out answers from others and not trusting my intuition or approaches. In doing so, I am critical and judgmental of my capability and rely on the capacity of others, consequently deeming my own solution not as valuable as that of another.

We can't forget that we are social beings and that our natural preference is to be liked. While our continued survival is now less dependent on being part of a group, it is still very much a part of our lives and our biology. Remember that social exclusion and negative comparisons for the brain are almost akin to physical pain. From early school days, we are aware of the subgroups that exist in a school community and which group we want to be a part of, or not be associated with. But before we get to school, our ways of relating to others have already begun to be cemented by the relationships we have with our parents or caregivers.

If comparison is the fertiliser, then a bed of insecurity will naturally be filled with Lacking-based relationships that grow and feed on each other. A person's Lacking sense of self will match up with people who support and agree with this view. If I believe X, I will gravitate towards others who also share this view of X, whether that be consciously or unconsciously.

REFLECTION TASK FIFTEEN

1. Make a list of the qualities that you associate with being a secure person. Sometimes it can help to think of what you would identify with an insecure person, then list its opposite. For example, an insecure person might doubt their decisions, actions, or ability. A secure person would therefore believe in their decisions, actions, or ability.

2. Choose one of those qualities.

3. Complete the table below to expand on what you would be thinking, feeling, and doing when your chosen quality is in action.

Thinking	Feeling	Doing

This scale is very much about perceptions of the Self and perceptions of others. When insecurity is in action, it may look like other characteristics of the Lacking, as some of the other scales depict what might be happening when leaning towards an insecure state of being.

Anything I do, say, think, feel, or believe is because of how I want to be perceived or think I should be perceived.

The Lacking side of this scale is the embodiment of the fear that my true essence is not good enough:

to be accepted by others
to be accepted by me.

The Scales

> Criticism ←——→ Respect
>
> On the left, the others are wrong, and I have to tell them.
>
> On the right, we find acceptance of others and their differences.

Here is what I might be thinking, saying, or focusing on in the critical stance:

My way is better.
I can't believe they don't get it.
I have more experience.
You don't listen to instructions.
You're incompetent.
I can't believe I did that.
I did it again!
They are all idiots.
I'm so stupid.

If you look at the examples above, many relate to the Other. The spotlight is on them under a What's Wrong lens, where it's expressed or implied that the Self is stronger or better.

When reversed, the spotlight falls on the Self under the What's Wrong lens and shows as self-criticism, and the Other sets the standard—what is right, whether it's expressed or implied. I say 'implied', as if I am critical of myself, it is because I believe I have done something wrong—that my acts or omissions are not good enough. If this is the case, it's because there is a right way to do things, something that I haven't done. I haven't done it right, yet others have. Given there are two characters, here if the Self is wrong, the Other must be right.

> **If I am wrong, you must be right.**
> **If you are wrong, I must be right.**

Have you ever found yourself criticising someone for something, only to later realise you're doing the exact same thing? What I noticed personally is that when I criticise others, it's normally an outward reflection of something I don't like in myself. Perhaps that's why it irritates me so much to see others doing it, or why I can even see it in the first place.

Closely linked to insecurity, I criticise others because it increases my worth and diverts the attention to the shortfalls of the Other. That is a diversion from my true essence, which includes both my strengths and weaknesses.

'I should have…'

'I wish I'd…'

'I can't believe I…'

Sound familiar? Those conversations with the Self that zoom in on What's Wrong, making you feel shame, remorse, or regret. This is where you play the role of the villain, outcast, or loser. These are less obvious because no one else witnesses these conversations, yet they are just as heavy as those with others. They point to a lack of respect for the person you are today, usually in comparison to others.

In a workplace environment, criticism can play out as being dismissive of a colleague's work or input or the general nitpicking that could easily roll into workplace harassment. The hierarchical nature of most workplaces leaves them open to abuse of power. In reality, in any relationship with any level of reliance, there is the possibility of a power imbalance. In this scale, the presence of a power imbalance makes the criticism heavier.

The competing interests might include:

Nothing and no-one is ever good enough	**Versus**	respecting and accepting differences.

I am not good enough	**Versus**	respecting and accepting myself.

REFLECTION TASK SIXTEEN

1. Think about what respect means to you.
2. How do you know that you are being respected?
3. Make a list of qualities that you associate with being respected.
4. Choose one of those qualities.
5. Complete the table below to expand on what you would be thinking, feeling, and doing when your chosen quality is in action.

Thinking	Feeling	Doing

In this scale, The Lacking shows up as disrespect because when you criticise, respect is missing. That's not to say that you can't have an opinion. A difference of opinion can exist with or without respect. To have an opinion is to hold a particular view on a subject where there may be others who share this view and others who do not. Each can exist.

    Can I allow others to hold an opinion that I do not without feeling as though my opinion is wrong or questioning my view?
Or, conversely, without feeling as though their opinion is wrong and being compelled to correct or impose my view on them?

    This scale is about those interactions that divert attention to a Lacking, with the Self or Other.
The fear behind the criticism is that my true essence is not good enough:

without showing others where they lack
highlighting where I lack.

The Scales

> Victim ⇔ Survivor
>
> On the left is the 'Why me?' approach.
>
> On the right, strength.

Terrible things happen every day to people and children all over the world. Events that can take years of therapy and healing and healthy relationships to resolve. I am by no means minimising the impact of trauma and abuse. What I am focusing on here is the hidden day-to-day victim mode that may not be a result of just one or even a series of events. I'm talking about patterns we can all fall into as life happens. Approaches that can block us from having meaningful relationships, progressing our careers, or generally moving forward in life. Are we going to overcome or be overcome?

What I might be thinking, saying, or focusing on in the victim stance:

I'm the sick one.
Bad things always happen to me.
I'm always last in the queue.
I'll never get that job because I'm not the favourite.
Bad luck finds me.
I can't X because of Y.

Anyone raised in an environment with a strong negative bias may find themselves swimming against the current to shake this one off. It's another scale that uses comparison, where the Other is always luckier, prettier, richer, better, and generally has a much easier life. If the Other is up, then I am down.

The 'Why me?' stance is where the Self experiences a Lacking while the Other experiences Strength. It can be expressed or implied, as it places the spotlight on the Other by highlighting, from a What's Wrong lens, what the Self does not have or can't do. Remember, comparison, for the brain, is almost the same as physical pain.

Show me a potentially positive outcome, and I'll shoot it down with a list of reasons why it won't pan out for me. Or I'll be the silent victim and tell myself that a positive outcome is possible and do whatever I have to do, like put in a job application, yet deep down, whether I realise it or not, I don't believe it's possible, and this disbelief comes through loud and clear in the job interview.

There is a multidimensional aspect. What is the quality of my corresponding thoughts, feelings, and actions?
This lens can become a part of identity and the perspective of self. If I'm not the unlucky, single, or funny one, then who am I?
It might also be expressed as a belief that things don't turn out for me and they never do because of an external factor. Or that things will turn out for me once an external factor takes place.

The competing interest might include:

I'll show you why I can't	**Versus**	why I can.
My default story	**Versus**	an unknown and unscripted narrative.
What's Wrong	**Versus**	What's Strong.

Like some of the other scales, it's me versus the world in which I take three steps forward and ten steps back and, no matter what, I'm destined to fail or be worse off than everybody else. I won't get that promotion, apartment, goal weight, partner, holiday…because it just never works out for me. There's always an external factor that is out of my control stopping me.

I can't X because of Y

X = pay off my mortgage
Y = I don't have a partner to help pay it off

X = go on a holiday
Y = another colleague normally takes that month off

X = go on a big overseas trip
Y = I don't have anyone to go with

X = lose weight
Y = I can't afford to go to the gym

Sure, there are things we can't do for real, valid reasons; that's not what this is about. It's more the average and not-so-average everyday situations and challenges. There can also be an element of blame here, which is the topic of the next scale.

It is a sense that the Self will not succeed or achieve for a series of external material reasons, with a hint of negative comparison to others.

I won't be chosen because:

I don't have a master's degree—the Other with a master's degree will.

I'm too old—the Other person who is younger will.

I don't have the experience—the more experienced Other will.

I have a tainted past—the Other without a tainted past will.

I'm the slow one—the quicker Other person will.

I'm the single one—the Other in a relationship will.
I'm the unemployed one—the employed Other will.

Essentially the spotlight is on the Other, what the Other has or is doing or can do. When the spotlight is on the Other, the Self is being measured against the individuality of another. So to flip the scale, it's about shifting where the spotlight is facing. This change in focus moves the spotlight onto the goals, situation, individuality, and aspirations of the Self and not a third party.

The Victim lens expresses the fear that my true essence is not good enough:

to succeed or achieve
to be accepted by others
to let go of the past if I am no longer a victim.

REFLECTION TASK SEVENTEEN

1. Go back to the person you chose in Reflection Task One, on page 14 where you looked at the qualities shown by a survivor of adversity.

2. Choose one quality to explore in further detail. For example, determination.

3. Complete the table below with what you might be thinking, feeling, or doing when applying that chosen quality.

4. The following are some examples of what you might be thinking, feeling, or doing when applying the chosen quality of determination.

The Scales

Thinking	Feeling	Doing
I am going to do this. I can do this. I can work this out. I might also think about what it will be like when it's completed. I am focusing more on What's Strong and trying not to stay too long in What's Wrong thoughts when they come up.	*I feel determined, nervous, excited, confident, calm, some fear, forgiving of myself and others, proud, misunderstood, hopeful, willing, optimistic, thankful.*	*'I am proactive about what needs to be done. I keep getting back up when things don't go to plan. I look for potential options and information that may help. I might also be doing research, which might look like reading a book or watching YouTube clips or attending workshops or seminars that support my goals or situation. I might also have a routine to help me.'*

Blame ◄─────►	Empowerment
On the left, I will point the finger at others.	On the right, I accept my role in situations and events and embrace the lessons

Here is what I might be focusing on in the blame stance:

you
them
it.

Here is what I might be thinking or saying:

My hands are tied.
It's because of him/her/them.
If it wasn't for…

Finger pointing. I saw it all around me—the tendency to jump and blame someone else when things don't go as planned. Like criticism and victimhood, blame deflects away from the Self and turns the spotlight onto others. 'It's not me. I don't own it. It's not my problem. It's not me—it's you.'

It's those moments in life when something bad happens to me because of something someone else did, didn't do, or said. It's in these moments that it's all too easy to find fault in another and determine them as the cause of current turmoil or difficulties.

Deflecting parts of a situation that can be attached to another person, object, situation, or event—that is what this scale is addressing.

In doing so, the Self is being disempowered, handing over fault and responsibility to someone else, only to go further down victimhood and the 'I'm helpless' path. We disempower ourselves when we give away a potential learning opportunity by distancing ourselves from the situation and blaming another.

We learn from our mistakes, so in handing over responsibility to another via blame, we hand over our chance to learn and grow and do things differently. A potentially empowering opportunity becomes disempowering. These are missed opportunities for empowerment, learning, and growth.

Take, for example, this age-old excuse: The dog ate my homework. Let's look for the lessons here. What could I do next time to prevent this? What lessons, advice, or guidelines would I tell my future self to help avoid this scenario repeating? These always come from a strength-based perspective.

Is it a lesson in:

being proud of my work and abilities
knowing that it's okay to ask for help
making time and space for homework.

The competing interests might include:

Highlighting the role of another	**Versus**	acceptance of my role.
Deflection of my part	**Versus**	embracing the learnings.
Being disempowered	**Versus**	being empowered.

REFLECTION TASK EIGHTEEN

1. Find a space where you can walk uninterrupted for a few moments. It might be up and down a corridor, a flight of stairs, the street you live in, or a nearby park.

2. Take a moment to think about what empowerment means to you. Does it have a shape, sound, feel, colour, word, or texture?

3. Begin walking with empowerment.

4. With each step you take, sense that colour, sound, texture, shape, or word, strengthening with every stride as you practise walking with empowerment for a few moments.

> Judgement ←——→ Understanding
>
> On the left is the superior to others.
>
> On the right, we are open to and accepting of differences.

I might be thinking or saying:

That's not the way it's done.
I'd be so ashamed if that were me.
What a _____!
I have to just do it myself.
Everyone fails to meet my expectations.

I might be focusing on:

black-and-white thinking
jumping to conclusions
high expectations of self.

Judgement is what you feel when you walk away from someone who has a bad poker face and completely gives away what they think of you or your situation. It can result in a spiral of judgement, as being judged can all too easily result in a reciprocal barrage of judgmental thoughts or comments that sound like:

I can't believe she said that!
That is not what I expected of her.
How narrow-minded!
She must think I'm so shallow!

Judgement fuels judgement. In judgement, we impose our views onto the Other and, in some cases, we are the Other. The Self, judging the Self almost as it does to the Other. Like criticism, we focus on What's Wrong, as to criticise is to judge.

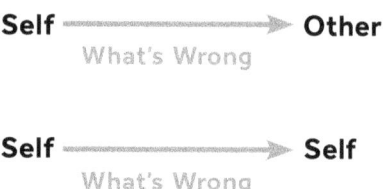

An alternate ending could see the person being judged agree with that judgement and continue to feature it in self-talk and negative self-analysis that might go on for days after the event.

Like criticism, it highlights the faults and flaws and What's Wrong in both the Self and the Other.

I know in myself that I am switching into judgement mode when I move from open questions to closed questions, which are often also leading questions. This is fine if you are a legal representative trying to win a case, not while discussing the recycling bin rules with your partner or flatmate.

Those conversations are crafted to catch someone out or to prove a point or, worse still, to prove someone else is inferior in some way. They are questions that often give away our thoughts about a situation and generally require a 'Yes' or 'No' answer.

The Scales

REFLECTION TASK NINETEEN

Read through these examples of open and closed questions. Rewrite the last four closed questions into open-questions.

Closed Questions	Open Questions
Do you eat pancakes for breakfast?	What do you eat for breakfast?
Did that make you angry?	How did that make you feel?
Could you have asked an open ended-question?	What else could you have asked?
Will you be going to your grandmother's for Christmas?	Where are you going for Christmas?
Did you think that the oven you purchased is the best choice?	What made you choose that oven?
Don't you think you should be staying at home tonight?	Do you have plans for tonight?
Are you feeling better today?	How do you feel today?
Do you get along well with your neighbour?	Tell me about your relationship with your neighbour.
Did you have a good trip?	How was your trip?
Do you take the train to work?	
Don't you think it's childish for you to act that way?	
Have you ever tried calorie counting?	
Will you be wearing that?	

The competing interests might include:

Black-and-white thinking	**Versus**	being open-minded with room for shades of grey.
Limited options	**Versus**	unlimited options.
What's Wrong	**Versus**	What's Strong.
High expectations for a situation	**Versus**	acceptance of a situation.
My view	**Versus**	acceptance of the views of Others.

Judgement reflects the value we place on both the Self and Other and points to a Lacking; I'm hard on myself, or I'm hard on others.

This is also the scale of unmet expectations. It's either black or white, with little room in between, and again, it's directed to both the Self and Others. Anything outside this is questioned or not good enough. Judged.

Whichever way you look at it, there's a sense of Lacking at the root of judgement. I find this scale a challenge, as our natural judgements can sneak in without us realising. Any time we are imposing our ideas onto another and not allowing them to simply be, that is judgement. Am I pushing my ideas and views onto the Other? Am I pushing my ideas and views on how I should be onto myself?

Judgement = What's Wrong and may appear as criticism, victimhood, blame, focusing on the past, denial, assumptions, or punishment.

Judgement fuels the fear that my true essence is not good enough and so I might:

point to the flaws in others instead, or
tend to highlight the flaws in myself, or
feel the need to prove that others are wrong, and I am right.

It's Not You, It's Me!

> Denial ←——→ Acceptance
>
> On the left is strong resistance and avoidance.   On the right, open acknowledgment.

Here is what I might be thinking, saying, or focusing on in the denial stance:

I avoid the issue, sometimes with a distraction.
I know that deflection is what I do best.
I often blame or criticise others.
I make promises I won't keep.
I will always have an explanation.
I minimise the situation.
I avoid a situation completely when I can.

Think of those brilliant plans that are made yet never executed. Any New Year's resolutions involving kickstarting your fitness routine or getting healthy are good examples.

> **Scenario:** I'm going to join a gym in winter because in summer I like to be outdoors and go for walks along the beach. It's still daylight when I get home from work, so I can go for a walk then. Winter arrives. It's too cold and gets dark early. I can't exercise outside. I'll join a gym in summer, when the days are longer. I feel better in summer; I'll do it then. Repeat.
>
> **My conclusion:** I'll do it later once the external conditions are better. I'm not ready now. I can't do it yet. I don't want to do it yet.
>
> **Result:** No action. No change. Familiarity and the known situation win; I'll never get fit.

REFLECTION TASK TWENTY

1. Rewrite the scenario above using the elements observed in those who triumphed over adversity in the table below.

2. What stands out to you as the most important element of this rewrite?

	Thinking	Feeling	Doing
Acceptance			
Forgiveness			
Future Focus			
Discipline			

Denial can also blur our vision and make looking in the mirror more challenging, as what we see is not always the most accurate representation of reality and can often divert focus onto the 'Other', a situation, or object. It can be more comfortable to avoid or deny what is happening because the reality is painful.

This could encompass those situations that force us into survival mode to prevent a major collapse. The only way our bodies can physically continue is by turning the volume way down. Let's face it; bad things happen while life continues around us, and we do what is necessary in that moment until that moment becomes the continuing future. That's when denial can take over with a life of its own.

Scenario: My relationship ended, but I've got work to do, so I'll park that sadness, disappointment, rejection, and fear until later. I tell myself, 'I'm okay. I never loved him anyway. It wasn't meant to be,' and I put the volume down like that, almost entirely muting the pain of the situation.

My conclusion: I am not good at relationships, and that's just how I am, or the belief that I'm not good enough to be in a relationship or to be loved.

Result: Little or no acknowledgement of the situation, covered by explanations, distractions, avoidance, and pouring energy into other commitments.

The competing interests might include:

Muting my reality	**Versus**	confronting the discomfort and pain.
Deflecting onto others	**Versus**	looking in the mirror.
'I always have an explanation'	**Versus**	acceptance of the situation.
'I'm okay'	**Versus**	'I'm actually not okay with the situation'.

It's removing the Self from discomfort so as not to be affected by it. Removal can look like avoidance, deflection, broken promises, addiction, or explanations that can act as valid excuses.

Denial hides the fear that my true essence is not good enough:

to be accepted by others for who I am
because my experience is sad and uncomfortable
because I am in pain
for me to accept myself.

> Past ←——→ Future
>
> On the left, the focus is on old events, people, situations.
> On the right the attention is on the present with a future focus.

I might be:

placing greater emphasis on past events than the present
holding grudges
finding it hard to forgive those who hurt me
reluctant to try new things.

I might be focusing on:

wishful thinking about the good old days
regretting my actions.

In relationships, past hurts can often inform present and future ones and can look like:

no other relationship matching up to a past one
difficulty trusting a new partner because of the actions of a former partner
not allowing a new partner to enter because of past hurts.

These apply equally to all kinds of relationships—with friends, colleagues, family, acquaintances. This scale goes hand in hand with forgiveness, just as staying in past hurts holds those past unforgiven situations in the present day. It holds us stuck in the past in a way in which we can justify our thoughts, feelings, and actions. It could also take the form of negative bias and recollections of the past that become the default perspective and prevent present situations from forming or flowing.

The competing interests might include:

Holding onto past hurts	**Versus**	forgiving and releasing past hurts.
Staying in the familiar good old days	**Versus**	embracing the present and walking into the future.
Sitting in certainty	**Versus**	leaping towards the unknown.

Biologically, it's natural to stick to what we know. It's predictable and can feel safer. It's how we've survived as a species, recognising and remembering dangers or threats to be ready for and prevent their return.

When I reflect on the examples of survivors of adversity, one of the elements that jumped out to me was having a future focus, which required a releasing of the past. This was also true for people I observed as successful in many areas of their life; they were always moving forward with new ideas and approaches—wanting to improve, grow, try different ways, and keep the past in the past. They looked forward to new opportunities because they believed in themselves and saw what was possible, and they kept the spotlight on them—as opposed to the persons who wronged them or situations that didn't go to plan.

The Lacking end of this scale does the opposite; it keeps past events, people, or situations, both good and bad, in the present.

It's Not You, It's Me!

In remaining in this past stance, I nourish the fear that my true essence is not good enough:
without the story of my past experiences
because I made mistakes in the past
because I was harmed by others in the past.

> **REFLECTION TASK TWENTY-ONE**
>
> 1. On a blank piece of paper, draw a line with an arrow on either end.
>
> 2. On the left, write PAST; on the right, write FUTURE. Then choose a point in between and write PRESENT.
>
>
>
> **Past**　　　　　Present　　　　　**Future**
>
> 3. Choose a small object—it might be a paperclip, a crystal, a pen, or a button—that you can place on the line on that piece of paper.
>
> 4. Now think of a time when you have been hurt, disappointed, or upset by someone, a group, or a situation. Choose a scenario where the emotions aren't as intense as they have been but are still present and felt.
>
> 5. Use the small item to plot on the paper where in time you feel that event is sitting for you now.
>
> 6. Make a list of the Strength-based learnings that have arisen from this situation.
> **Examples:**
> *I focus on my strengths.*
> *I choose to accept myself for who I am and all my past versions for who they were.*
> *I accept the past and leave it in the past.*

I choose not to take things personally.
It's okay to seek advice from people who can help me.
This has taught me that I am worthy of friends who appreciate me for who I am.

7. Go back to the timeline and review the placement of the object. Where does it sit?

8. Are there any new learnings or clues for you to take from the placement of the object?

Assumption ⟷	Evidence
On the left, we accept Lacking or Strength without proof.	On the right, we rely on real information and proof.

What I might be thinking, saying, or focusing on:

I bet they are talking about me.
I'm going to lose.
I just know that she wants my job.
I won't get promoted, so I'm not going to apply.
They are going to rip me off, I know it!

When I say assumptions, I especially mean the ones that place the Self in the Lacking at the hands of others. They can often come disguised as intuition or a gut feeling that something terribly wrong is about to happen. Sometimes it is intuition, while other times—and more often than not—it's simply jumping to negative conclusions based on an interpretation of events that leans towards an internal fear or Lacking—a Lacking that can completely overtake intuition while cunningly presenting as a gut feeling.

Scenario One: I can recall a recent time when I had convinced myself of an outcome that involved me reaching conclusions about someone that, of course, weren't very good. I had filled in the gaps from my own lens, the Lacking lens.

My Conclusion: I was deadset certain that my hypothesis was correct and was consequently utterly disappointed and upset with someone despite the absence of tangible evidence.

Result: An unexpected turn of events meant that I was privy to new information that completely exposed my Lacking-based assumptions and the insecurity that led me to make them.

I got it completely wrong. So wrong. The actual facts, I honestly can't remember. What stayed with me was the feeling of 'Holy crap, I took things way too far in my head.' I felt so embarrassed and ashamed that my judgement, insecurity, fear—you name it—all came out that day, and it was completely unjustified. Yet it was super easy to do. It made me wonder about the times when I didn't get the extra information, the missing piece of the puzzle that would have made everything crystal clear, those times when I accepted a completely made-up negative situation. How many other times had I made an assumption that essentially highlighted what I didn't have or what someone was trying or going to take away from me?

This lens gives the author creative freedom to react to the Lacking as they please, with limited details or evidence.

It's Not You, It's Me!

> **Scenario Two:** A group of friends, all dressed up and ready for a fun night out. The location is one of those funky, new, inner-city bars with mix-matched décor that just works. The barmen are super cool, most with beards, and the latest music is playing loudly through all the speakers. So loud that any kind of communication is restricted to screaming into the ear of the person next to you. One woman turns to the friend closest to her and leans into her ear to tell her as loudly as she can that she is going to get a drink. The next minute, one of the other women runs out in a huff. She eventually tells the friend who chased after her that she is sick of everyone talking about her.
>
> **Her Conclusion:** 'Everyone is talking about me.'
>
> **Result:** A distorted view of the situation at the hands of assumptions taken as fact. Ones that originate in self-Lacking and point the finger at the Other.

The competing interests might include:

| Jumping to Lacking-fuelled conclusions | **Versus** | responding to all the information at hand. |

Again, this scale had elements of both the Self and others. I draw conclusions based on what I might lose at the hands of others and jump in for a preventative strike to do what I can to stop the situation from happening.

Assumptions can serve to hide while also enforcing the fear that my true essence is not good enough:

to be accepted by others
because the other's true essence is more valuable than mine
for me to simply accept myself.

REFLECTION TASK TWENTY-TWO

Consider Scenario Two and complete the table below, firstly based on the event—the negative assumption—and then rewritten from the What's Strong lens.

	Thinking	Feeling	Doing
Negative Assumption			
What's Strong re-write			

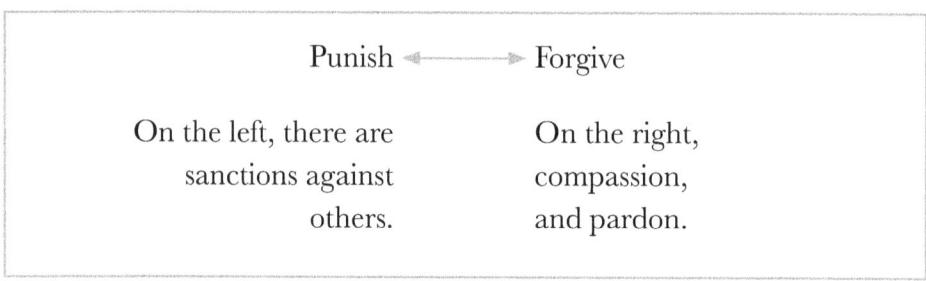

What I might be thinking, saying, or focusing on:

I'll get them back.
I won't forget this.
They will pay.

It's the 'You hurt me, so I'll hurt you' schoolyard fight scene. Hurting another who has hurt you and holding on to those hurts for dear life. In relationships of varying forms, it can look like:

not answering calls or messages
cut-offs
revenge
the black and white approach – inability to compromise or apply flexibility
avoidance
'You disagreed with me, so now I will disagree with you.'
'You left me, so now I won't be compromising here.'
'Take me to court; I'm not budging.'
'I'll take you to court; I'm not budging.'

    This is something I saw in the mediations. Tit-for-tat. You harmed me, so now I'll harm you. It would often mean that the needs and interests of the family as a whole were put out in some way. In much the same way, the individual lens zooms in on the needs and concerns of one person within a group. 'You disagreed with me on X, so now I won't agree with you on Y.'

The competing interests might include:

'You hurt me, and I won't let you forget it'	**Versus**	letting go of past hurts.
Being in control of the situation	**Versus**	detachment from the situation.
Past	**Versus**	future.

In punishing others, we feed the discomfort we are trying to avoid or lessen. The negativity poured onto those who harmed us hurts us more than it hurts them because there is freedom in forgiving, as it allows us to release and step into new experiences—new and unfamiliar experiences that we might not have much control over. This is also a scale that lives in the past and can make moving forward feel like walking in quicksand, keeping us in a familiar situation.

In holding a grudge or pursuing revenge, we keep ourselves closer to past events than our present or potential future. In the punishment stance, I fear that my true essence is not good enough:

without this hurt story
if I forgive and accept the situation
because this happened to me
because the actions of another hurt me.

REFLECTION TASK TWENTY-THREE

An opportunity to let forgiveness in.

1. Find a space where you can walk uninterrupted for a few moments. It might be up and down a corridor, a flight of stairs, the street you live in, or a nearby park.
2. Take a moment to think about what forgiveness means to you. Does it have a shape, sound, feel, colour, word, or texture?
3. Begin walking with forgiveness.
4. With each step you take, sense that colour, sound, texture, shape, or word, strengthening with every stride as you practise walking with forgiveness for a few moments.

The updated ladder provides a structured starting point for self-reflection with many overlaps that continually pointed back to the first two scales and a deficit of self. The additional scales add meaning and more detailed illustrations to the first two.

Updated Ladder of the Scales of Self-Reflection

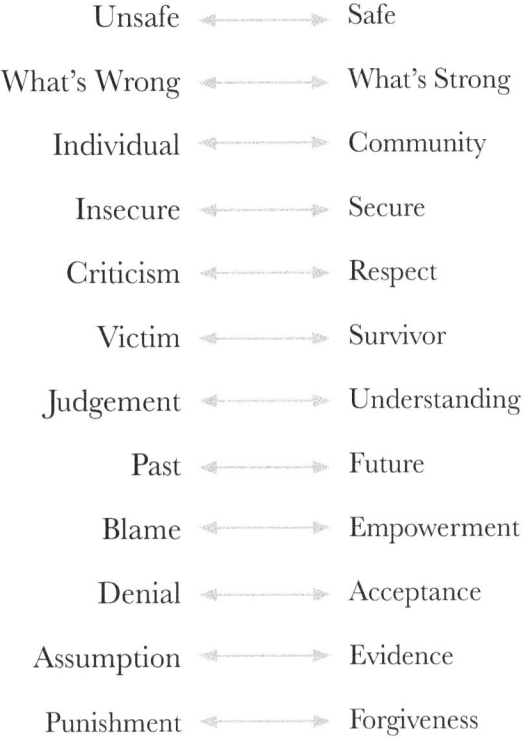

Evolution and our social nature have played their part. We respond the way we do as a survival mechanism, with adaptations to our experience forming our memories and default ways of responding. They inform our place on the ladder of scales as well as the conditions in place that would get us moving from one side of it to the other.

If your experience was sitting predominantly towards the right, towards What's Strong, it would mean that your relationships showed 'warmth', resilience was formed, and you may be less guided or overrun by Lacking. Yet, sadly, this is not always the case. There are no set rules or reasons to determine why on one day, we go one way, and on another day, we go another way. It's both important and helpful to acknowledge and support the impact and role had by our lived experience, our childhood experience in particular, something that differs greatly from person to person and this is explored in the next chapter.

CHAPTER 6

THE EXPERIENCE

My exploration of the topic of child development alongside my work served to further cement the significance and influence of the childhood experience. We are adaptations of our experiences. I witnessed the effect the quality of the parents' relationship has on a child's wellbeing, and I was trained to preach about the potential dangers of unresolved parental conflict on children—that it's not separation but the presence of unresolved parental conflict that can have a detrimental impact on a child's mental wellbeing.[28]

      My comments on families and separation assume that there are no safety concerns or danger, like forms of abuse and violence, that most would consider wrong, immoral, and unacceptable, a belief reflected by the local laws.

I learnt to view consistently unresolved parental conflict as a form of emotional abuse or adversity. Its consequences are often misunderstood by society and go without the recognition or consideration given to other types of abuse, yet its impact could be just as debilitating. Anxiety, depression, post-traumatic stress symptoms, anger, as well as physical symptoms are some of the ways interparental conflict can impact children and grow with them into adulthood.[29]

      Any event that has potentially negative ramifications on one's emotional wellbeing is worthy of being acknowledged, supported, and resolved in some way, regardless of the label or category it has been given or not given. It's less about the situation and more about the impact on the person. What if, for example, we are dealing with a highly sensitive child?[30] How might they be impacted, and what kind of support will this child need in comparison with another child of the same age?

This is what I was seeing more and more in mediations. I wondered whether there had been a substantial increase in the number of highly sensitive children in the last ten years, or was it merely the fact that our society had become more aware?

This brings me to one of the most consequential observations of my career—it's not the specific details or gravity of an event or situation but the gravity that event or situation has had on the individual.

As for unresolved parental conflict, in my eyes it's a form of silent child abuse, an adverse, traumatic experience that can have lifelong impacts. I say 'silent' because I believe it is without the due attention and support that it deserves.

These traumatic experiences, if not supported and processed appropriately, can ripple into and devastate lives. Addiction, mental health issues, relationship issues, physical conditions, emotional ill health, depression, and self-harm are some of the potential outcomes.[31]

Traumatic events that live and breathe and grow in our bodies may make the approach I am proposing challenging or unpleasant. Perhaps even the title of this book may seem to minimise the impact of abuse by others. That's not my intention.

Unprocessed trauma makes life harder because the starting point is always many steps behind everybody else. Catching up alone is not easy. The right support can prove invaluable. I strongly encourage anyone reading this who is carrying sad and unacceptable events of the past within them to seek out the services of those dedicated to working with others to lessen the load.

Science tells us that the childhood experience is a learning opportunity in which our brains are gathering information and forming patterns and memories that will guide future interactions and expectations.[32] We are learning which side of the scale to lean towards from a young age, and by adulthood, these ways of being are cemented into our bodies.

Cement—a solid and long-lasting building material used to hold foundations in place. One that is very difficult to remove or move without assistance once it has been set.

When we are born, we are not fully developed. We cannot walk, eat, or talk, so our survival depends on our caregivers and the relationship we have with them. These all help form us into the people we become. Some of our childhood experiences lean towards What's Strong while others lean towards What's Wrong. These experiences, combined with our genes, direct and guide our development and learning, including our knowledge of the world, what to expect from it, how we will respond, and what we need to do to survive.[33] Whether we would show resilience or vulnerability when faced with adversity would be determined by our experience and our genes. I saw this knowledge in the form of a scale, one with biological (genes) and physical (experience) variables that would determine which side we leaned towards.

Vulnerable ◄─────► Resilient

Yet epigenetics tells us that our genes could be turned on or off by our experiences and were consequently not, as once thought, set in stone.[34]

Experience + Genes = Outcome
(yet Genes could be altered by Experience).
Outcome = default scales.

Our physical experience can modify our biology; it is not only influential, but it can also enact change. Again, the weight of our experience—our early experiences, in particular—cannot be underestimated or ignored. Our family of origin.

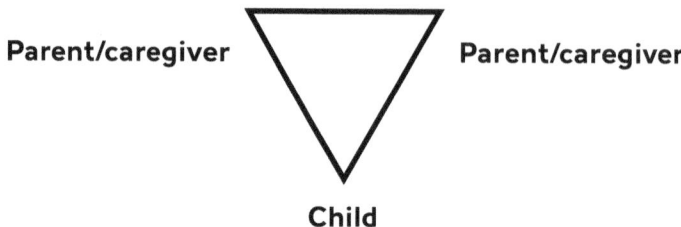

Drawing from my studies in family therapy meant that I often viewed relationships in the form of triangles, a concept used in family therapy.35 While this notion has had several forms and adaptations from various models of therapy, what I took from it was the ease in which the dynamics between three people could be illustrated using a shape.36

If you look at a triangle as a structure, it becomes a shape in which each side has an impact on the other.

In the application of this idea, I refer to families where there are no safety concerns, harm, or abuse. While I am proposing that unresolved parental conflict is a form of emotional abuse, if I called the police or relevant authority to say that I just witnessed a set of parents being critical and spiteful towards each other in front of their children, this would not set off any alarm bells.

It would go largely unnoticed simply because the situation doesn't fall within a prescribed form that would call for immediate intervention. Yet there is an obvious impact, which my work and a substantial amount of research exposed me to daily.37

Going back to the triangle, each side contributes to a child's development and learning as a large part of the experience component.

While there is an abundance of research and theories on child development and the parental influence, here I am relying on two components that influence and mould child development, the experience and the genes, that work alongside the notion that we—or rather what we do, think, say or show—are adaptations to our experience.

Were these experiences predominately highlighting What's Wrong or What's Strong?

Merging the scales with the triangle, we can now see each side in the triangle is either leaning towards What's Wrong or What's Strong, determining the quality and strength of each side. What's Wrong is lacking and What's Strong is strength. Is it solid and straight or fragmented? What does the integrity of one side mean for the others?

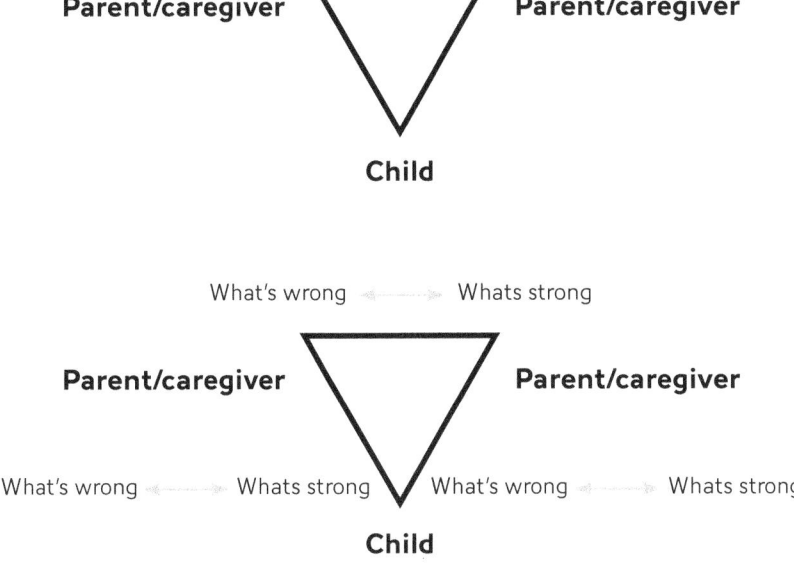

In using the triangle as a representation of the first triangle a child belongs to, this shape doubles as a classroom—the learning environment. A place where the child is receiving many messages through the observations of their parents or caregivers, messages that become integrated into their physical, social, and emotional development.
These are messages about relating with:

the Self
the Other.

Messages may evolve into a way of being in which the dominant lens becomes the default and infiltrates all aspects of being and relating with the Other and the Self.

A What's Wrong default lens for the Self might look like any interaction or response where the Self is less than the Other, which may manifest as relationships with the Other and the Self that support this view.

Conversely, a What's Wrong default lens for the Other might look like any interaction or response where the Other is less than the Self, which may manifest as relationships with the Other and the Self that support this view.

From an early age, the child is learning which end of the scale it's safe to stay on. It may be that our childhood experience has taught us to view life from the left side of the scale because that was the example we were shown, and our survival demanded it.

It's only right and fair to acknowledge the impact the triangle we grew up in has had on us and to do so in a productive way. Your triangle will establish norms—the default lens. What's Wrong or What's Strong, which is the first duality. The second duality is the characters. There are always two:

The Self—I see What's Wrong/Strong in myself.
The Other—I see What's Wrong/Strong in others.

The What's Wrong lens can all too easily move into criticism, blame, judgement, negative assumptions, a focus on past situations, and victim mode, and may result in the 'I'm not good enough' mode, making self-reflection a challenge and risk mutating into negative self-talk.

It's hard to always get it right as a parent—a parent who once was a child in a triangle—and it's equally hard to process and unlearn these experiences as an adult.

We haven't all come from the same starting point, and where we started will impact where we go and how we get there. Many amazing practitioners do marvellous work and research on processing childhood experiences. I add this note here because in proposing the idea of the scales of self-reflection, it is vital to acknowledge the challenges and the need for a wide-angle lens, one that includes and appreciates the bigger picture. The scales of self-reflection will only be as relevant or useful as the lens they are viewed with, yet the lens can vary and be greatly affected by our experience.

A wide-angle, strengths-based approach explores the childhood experience with compassion.
This might look like obtaining assistance from people who are trained to do so, whether through traditional or non-traditional forms. Your journey will be unique to your own experience and guide you towards the services, information, support, lifestyle, or activities that will work for you and with you.

Remember to be kind to yourself as you go along on your journey.

REFLECTION TASK TWENTY-FOUR

Write a strengths-based I AM affirmation that resonates with you and respects your experience.
You could use the scales as a base, for example:

I am love and understanding.
I am strength.
I am resilient.
I am forgiving.

CHAPTER 7

THE SCALES IN PRACTICE

In practice, the scales provided a kickboard into self-reflection, yet this process could all too easily be hijacked by rumination and self-criticism, deviating completely from the purpose of both self-reflection and the scales. Some guidance could perhaps offer a strength-based check-in to help stay on the path of reflection and learning.

Drawing on some of the elements of the Strength and my observations of those who have triumphed in the face of adversity in the Lacking chapter, the guidelines for using the scales of self-reflection emerge:

>   forgiveness—show
>   acceptance—welcome
>   respect—hold
>   love—apply.

Love—it was the goal, the overarching principle behind all the elements of the Strength, so it was only natural that it forms part of the guidelines. To show love was to respond with understanding, respect, forgiveness and to do so in a manner that looked towards the future—to focus on What's Strong.

The guidelines are designed to aid reflection in a way that encourages growth and highlights strengths while avoiding rumination, self-criticism, and shame. They call for gentle internal honesty with oneself in a world that focuses on external standards and comparisons. Something that does not always come naturally and can be easier on one day and harder on the next.

The gulf between understanding an idea and living it is vital here, and it is a continuing challenge for me.

The reality is that if we find ourselves analysing our thoughts, feelings, or actions, then chances are it's because they are leading towards the Lacking. These thoughts and feelings are likely to be heavy and dense, and they open the door to over-thinking, doubt, and confusion while acting as a major clue that you are leaning towards the Lacking. When heading towards the Strength, we are more likely to encounter thoughts and feelings that are much lighter with less urge to analyse.

When the Lacking lens dominates our view, these guidelines can be used to encourage and shape a rewrite towards the Strength.

You can follow this guide, yet if you aren't 'living it' in a multi-dimensional way, then gaps or inconsistencies will continue to pop up in certain parts of your life.

Let's look at making a negative assumption in exploring how to use the guidelines. Has there been a time that you jumped to conclusions about a situation—made a negative assumption? You can also refer to the scenarios explored in the assumption/evidence scale on pages 89 and 90. What is the quality of our thoughts, feelings, and actions when making a negative assumption?

For many, articulating the actual feeling or emotion doesn't come naturally, so it might help to consider it from the point of view of the body. Is there a sensation in your body that can offer you a clue about the quality of the feelings you have towards a situation?

The table below is a written example of using the guidelines to support a rewrite and extract the lessons from making a negative assumption.

Negative Assumption	Thoughts	Feelings	Actions
Forgiveness	It's ok, I have learnt from this	Relief, peace light	Moving forward with the lessons. I am kind to myself
Acceptance	It happened. So be it	Open, calm and caring	I will take these lessons to future situations. I am more aware when I make assumptions
Respect	I can see how this happened. There are learnings from this.	Worthy patient	I show understanding, kindness and non-judgement to myself
Love	All of the above	Compassion, trust, and safe	I acknowledge and release the embarrassment or shame and show gratitude for this lesson and growth opportunity.

This multidimensional aspect meant that if you didn't have all three in the Strengths mode—a trifecta—the odds were against you. If I was doing everything right and followed my morning rituals with militant discipline and consistency, but nothing changed, what was preventing or slowing a rewrite?

The answer is to look at the quality of all your thoughts, feelings, and actions, as they can offer valuable clues if any are leaning towards What's Wrong. They often show up in real life as repeat situations, blockages, or challenges. These are what I refer to as missed or delayed opportunities.

It's Not You, It's Me!

REFLECTION TASK TWENTY-FIVE

1. Pick one characteristic of the Lacking that feels or sounds familiar to you.

2. Have that Lacking in your mind and choose a situation where it played out.

3. Complete the table below with your chosen situation to show what would be happening if you were applying the guidelines in your approach to yourself in that situation.

If the situation included other people or organisations, have a try at filling in the table in relation to your thoughts, feelings, and actions towards those others.

	Show Forgiveness	Welcome Acceptance	Hold Respect	Apply Love
Think It				
Feel It				
Show It				

In addition to these guidelines, below are some practices that can be used as a way to incorporate the scales in day-to-day living.

Meditation

I have, for many years, felt the benefits of regular meditative practice, and I experience a sort of withdrawal when I stop. Symptoms include increased irritability and sensitivity with a lower threshold of reactivity. While I am generally patient and calm, periods without meditation diminish these qualities. I have now come to see meditation as a form of mental exercise. While the results weren't as tangible as with physical exercise and training, a Massachusetts General Hospital and Harvard Medical School neuroscientist, Sara Lazar, found that meditation resulted in structural changes in the brain. Her research showed that meditation helps strengthen the areas of the brain that you want to build up and tones down the parts you want to reduce; toning down the fear, anxiety, and stress while strengthening learning, memory, emotional regulation, perspective-taking, compassion, and empathy.[38] The more we practise, the more we change the structure of our brain in ways that are going to improve self-reflection and enable us to use the scales.

A scales-inspired meditation is one that I call the release relax meditation: release the Lacking, relax into strength. The release/relax meditation can easily be incorporated into your chosen scale.

You can use whichever combination is relevant and works for you or use your own. The idea is that you choose a scale or a combination that is important to you to become your focus during the meditation. With each breath, you release the Lacking and relax into the Strength.
Examples:

Release fear		Release judgement		Release criticism
Relax into	OR	Relax into	OR	Relax into
love		understanding		respect

I suggest that you read through the guide a few times before you begin to familiarise yourself with the meditation.

Again, the guidelines can help in supporting and encouraging regular practice. Sometimes it will flow, while other times it won't. It may take time to get into a rhythm that works. Show forgiveness, welcome acceptance, hold respect, and apply love to yourself during this journey.

Release/Relax Meditation

Get into a comfortable position, seated or lying down.

Close your eyes and take a few slow and long breaths. To begin, breathe in the Strength and breathe out the Lacking and repeat as you continue to breathe.

For example:

**breathe in—relax into respect
breathe out—release criticism.**

Continue this practice for a few moments.

Visualisation: Infusion of Love

This started as a morning practice shortly after I had an iron infusion that got me thinking: Why can't I have other infusions? And so the infusion of love was born.

The idea is to imagine bringing love into your body—to visualise yourself receiving an infusion of love. It can begin at the tips of your toes and make its way to the top of your head via your choice of medium. For example, the love could emanate from the sun, moon, a beam of light, a waterfall, the waves of the ocean, the earth—any source that feels right for you.

Using the sun, a ray of light would start to cover your body, infusing you with love until your entire body has been infused.

Using the moon, it would be a moonbeam.

If you use the image of a waterfall, you could be walking or swimming under it.

It's really about choosing a source that resonates and is relevant for you.

It can be a quick practice, taking only a few minutes to start the day as you wake up in bed, or it can be a longer one.

I sometimes use this first thing in the morning before getting out of bed.

To begin the infusion:

1. Choose your source.

2. Get into a comfortable position, seated or lying down.

3. Close your eyes and take a few slow and long breaths.

4. Begin to visualise your chosen source infusing your body with love, starting at the feet and making its way to the top of your head.

5. Let the love infuse your body and give any part of your body that is sore or needs extra attention an additional, longer dose.

6. When you feel the infusion is complete, open your eyes and return to your day, fully infused.

While it is called an infusion of love, you could use other characteristics of the Strength or other words that lean towards love. For example:

infusion of strength
infusion of forgiveness
infusion of kindness
infusion of courage.

Example infusion of love using the rising sun:

To start, get into a comfortable position, seated or lying down.

Begin by taking a few slow long breaths and closing your eyes.

Imagine yourself lying down at your favourite beach as the sun begins to rise.

You feel the tips of your toes blanketed in the sun's warmth, infusing your feet with love, which gradually travels up your body, giving you a total infusion of love.

You lay here in this complete infusion of love that has spread into every part of you.

The love may stay a little longer or be more pronounced in areas of your body that are sore or unwell, as an extra dose is sent to these areas.

When your infusion is done, you can slowly return to your space in the present moment ready to continue your day with love.

Affirmations

Affirmations are a great way to highlight and emphasise What's Strong and set future goals. An easy place to start is an I AM affirmation inspired by the relevant scales. You could also use any strengths-based combination that is meaningful to you. What quality do you want to attach to your being to become your affirmation for the day?
Some examples:

I am love.
I am understanding.

**I am walking towards my future.
I am a survivor.**

Choose an affirmation that you believe in and that represents what is important to you. Write it in your planner. Memorise it. Say it aloud. Put it on a post-it note and keep it with you. Print it out and have it visible. Incorporate it into your daily ritual. In the end, the way you create and display it isn't as important as simply believing it in a multidimensional way.

The Day in Review

This practice is based on Rudolf Steiner's practice of retrospection, which, in very basic terms, asks that we review the events of the day by playing them backwards in our mind—something that can even be done in bed.[39]

Begin at the end of the day and then rewind. As you review your day backwards from end to beginning, pause at moments where you feel you could have done things differently, or anywhere the focus was on What's Wrong. The idea is to extract any valuable lessons rather than the specifics of the actual experiences of the day.

So, for example, if I blamed or criticised my partner/ friend/ parent in some situation, I would pause at that moment and replay that situation in my mind, re-scripting myself using the strengths lens, or What's Strong. It may also help to refer to the guidelines and show forgiveness, welcome acceptance, hold respect, and apply love to both the Self and others.

What I take from this practice is that it's the seemingly insignificant day-to-day events that can have a huge influence on open and honest self-reflection, as well as on genuine personal growth. This practice can provide valuable lessons that are completely self-guided and relevant to your experience and pace. Here are some prompts you can use to help draw out the learnings from this practice:

Reflect upon the rewrites of the day.
Can you see the point at which you went towards the Lacking?
What did you notice?

It's Not You, It's Me!

What about the moment that didn't require a rewrite?
Can you see the point where you stayed towards the Strength?
What did you notice?

This is a practice that can be done in bed at the end of the day and to bring awareness to the events of the day. It can be as structured and guided as you like because the value is in the outcome, which is the reflections and the associated lessons.

In the final chapter of It's Not You—It's Me, we will explore the tell-tale signs that you are headed on the road to the Lacking.

CHAPTER 8

IT'S NOT YOU, IT'S ME!

Hurdles to self-reflection—there are some, the biggest one being the Self during those moments when self-reflection mutates into overthinking and rumination.

I had already begun using some of the troubleshooting rules proposed in this chapter well before this book was even an idea. They helped keep me accountable and on track. All of which could be umbrellaed under 'It's not you—it's me'.

An instant self-check-in that could be applied to many common daily challenges. It places the focus inward where, at times, it's easier to shift the focus outwardly onto an external person, event or situation.

This chapter offers clues that we are leaning towards the Lacking. I say clues because looks can be deceptive, and I have found that it is all too easy to cross over to the Lacking while believing that you are heading towards the Strength. The devil is in the details.

The application of the 'It's not you—it's me' principle, as you will see below, is vital to making the flip towards the Strength: What's Strong. Many of the elements of my Lacking pointed the finger at another person, thing, or situation. Blamed another. Criticised another. Judged another. Someone or something was getting in the way and derailing me. It's where we can say 'It's not me—it's you!' and deflect Lacking onto an external factor.

My life. My attempts. My goals. All prevented, stopped, delayed, upset, or flipped at the hands of another. Someone is:

**upsetting me
stopping me
annoying me
offending me
forcing me
making me
delaying me.**

The other side of that is that if someone is the cause of disruption, disappointment, sadness, delay, and being unappreciated. Then does that mean that another person, place, situation, event, or thing is required to experience the opposite: flow, happiness, satisfaction and value?

If an external factor is the cause of discontent, does that mean that an external factor is required to feel content? This is where the external factor is the Other, the 'you' in 'It's not me—it's you!'

In reality, 'others' can cause hiccups and disruption, and it's something we don't have any control over. I'm not talking about abuse or dangerous behaviour; I mean the day-to-day dynamics of work, home, and friends, the dynamics with the guy on the bus, the woman at the supermarket, the comments made on social media—those sorts of things. Both simple and complex.

If we go back to the examples of those who overcame adversity in the Lacking chapter, some of them did experience abuse and severe hardship that gave them reasons to point the finger and blame another. Yet they remained in the What's Strong lens long enough for it to become their dominant lens and so they could focus on their future. They embodied 'It's not you—it's me', refusing to let external factors get in the way of their momentum and stepping into their future with forgiveness, acceptance, respect, and love.

These four concepts, combined with the 'It's not you—it's me' principle, create the troubleshooting guide below.

TROUBLESHOOTING GUIDE

Comparisons

Not only is the grass greener on the other side, it's also a huge meadow filled with fragrant flowers, birds, a pond, and bunny rabbits. It resembles a Monet painting. Making my side look like a frameless painting of a bunch of dying weeds and dried animal excrement.

The power of the characteristics of the Lacking can be dramatically amplified when comparing yourself to others. Something that, of course, I routinely did, and that would inevitably leave me with a void and a deficient self that would only continue to grow. One that would see me privately berate myself as I focused on my perceived shortcomings, or that would result in knee-jerk reactions.

I noticed that what I had done was place the spotlight on them—the others—while demoting myself to the shadows.

Why can the strength of another send us into Lacking and judgement of self? Here, we see the magnitude and impact of our perceptions and observations of the Other, leading to a deficiency of self in which the Other is the standard or measurement. The challenge is to catch ourselves out and apply the 'It's not you—it's me' principle, placing the spotlight back on the Self and using the self as a starting point.

This means we are measuring our achievements against the personal goals we have set for ourselves—as opposed to measuring our own achievements against those of others. This might also look like comparing your past self with your present self, placing the spotlight on your own growth and learning. In doing so:

> **show forgiveness**
> **welcome acceptance**
> **hold respect**
> **apply love...**

… to both the Self and others.

REFLECTION TASK TWENTY-SIX

1. Think of a time that you compared yourself to another.
2. Write down a few words to describe what you felt or thought during this comparison.
3. Did the comparison highlight a part of you that is wrong or strong?
4. If What's Wrong is being highlighted, complete the sentences below to show how you will apply the guidelines to this comparison:
   > I show forgiveness by…
   > I welcome acceptance by…
   > I hold respect by…
   > I apply love by…
5. Rewrite the comparison with the spotlight on you so it reflects your goals, interests, and choices. It might be a statement that confirms your strengths, current achievements, or something that you will strive to achieve. For example, 'I'm not as X as others' becomes:

I value, support, and grow my unique abilities and interests.
I choose to only compare myself to my younger self.
I am proud of how far I've come.
I love the way my determination helps me achieve my goals.
I strive to be the best version of me.

Inadmissible Evidence

Anyone who has ever watched any legal TV series or courtroom movie will be familiar with a courtroom scene in which two lawyers are fighting for victory and one attempts to submit evidence that backs up their case while the opposing lawyer seeks to have the evidence struck out. What is happening is less about the facts and more about the process. The evidence that is allowed to be relied upon and considered must comply with the rules of evidence.[40]

Very briefly, for evidence to be admitted, it needs to be verified by someone (a witness) or something (a document).

The witness can only attest to something they saw or heard themselves and not something they heard from someone else.

So they can only recall what they saw first-hand—their observations. Their opinions or assumptions about what they saw, while they might make interesting conversation, can't be used as evidence.

For example:

He was driving erratically = observation.
I think he was drunk = opinion or assumption.

Opinions and assumptions that would be inadmissible in court are a chronic overthinker's biggest weakness.

Assumptions: They are all too easy to make and can completely derail a situation or give it an entirely different meaning based on a hunch.

For example, I phoned John at his home, and he didn't answer the phone.

Assumption: He mustn't be home.
Can this be proven because John did not answer my call? No. Was John in the garden while the phone rang and didn't hear the phone ringing? Or was he in fact not at home? Only John knows.

It's Not You, It's Me!

Following the rules of evidence, anything that falls outside these rules is inadmissible evidence and cannot be submitted or relied upon.

The rules of evidence, I discovered, were the perfect aid to self-reflection for a chronic overthinker. The concept fascinated me, so much so that I shared it with many of my family and friends. It would routinely make an appearance when assumptions appeared, for assumptions, I noticed, were the seed and cause of much anxiety and stress, not just for me but particularly for anyone who would classify themselves as a chronic over-thinker. Not only were they unnecessary, but they had a tendency to lean towards the Lacking—jumping to conclusions that something bad was going to happen. A negative assumption could kickstart a series of actions to prevent or minimise its impact based on something that existed only in thought. It could cause unnecessary anxiety and stress and rely solely on inadmissible evidence.

In my version of the rules of evidence, if a thought is based on an assumption that is inadmissible in a court of law, perhaps it would be useful to reconsider how much weight and airtime we give it. The same goes for opinions and unsubstantiated gossip.

> **Scenario:** A young new member joins your office. They seem confident and know their work while expressing a willingness to learn and always say yes to work.
>
> **My conclusion:** While they don't actually do the same work I do and don't have the experience or qualifications that I have, I just know that they are working on taking over my job. I've seen the way they look at me and ask questions about my role, so I've started looking for another job. I'll leave before I get pushed aside.
>
> **Result:** I'm meeting with a recruiter later this week.

The 'It's not you—it's me' principle can be applied when jumping to conclusions that sound more like 'It's not me—it's you!', and the supporting evidence would definitely not be admitted in court.

It's Not You, It's Me!

This can be particularly difficult when our default setting is to prepare for and expect the worst-case scenario. For many, this is something that becomes ingrained at an early age. A traumatic event can emphasise the negative assumption default and negative bias, and it doesn't have to be an event that is experienced first-hand. It could be an event our parents or grandparents experienced that we 'inherited' biologically.[41] To demonstrate this, we can look to research into children of Holocaust survivors that found genetic alterations caused by a traumatic experience in both the parent and their offspring.[42] It is useful to keep this factor in mind and show compassion to yourself in this process, which is to witness with respect.

REFLECTION TASK TWENTY-SEVEN

When an assumption jumps in, how do you know? Apply the guidelines to the scenario described above to explore and flip the assumption by completing the table below.

	Show Forgiveness	Welcome Acceptance	Hold Respect	Apply Love
Think It				
Feel It				
Show It				

A Note About Intuition

I have often struggled to distinguish intuition and gut feelings from assumptions and fears that are soaked in Lacking. In those moments, the intensity of an assumption can feel a lot like intuition, with enough force to convince a sane and logical person to act on a whim. The assumption is likely to resemble judgements about other people or situations.

There is no set formula or rule for separating assumptions from intuition because, at times, these thoughts don't even dress like assumptions; they simply present as intuition. A clue can be the nature of the issue at hand. Is it going towards the Lacking or the Strength? While this is not always the best indicator, it's definitely a good place to start.

Essentially, if I find myself struggling with a particular situation or am simply uncertain about which way to go, it's the perfect time for intuition to step in. The problem is that my uncertainty is likely to have already steered me down the path of Lacking so that what I am sensing comes from a lens of the Lacking. What presents as intuition is riddled with What's Wrong and a general negative vibe with lots of reasons to back itself up. Intuition, by definition, is devoid of facts and evidence.

Those times I have felt lost and experienced difficulty making decisions, small or big, the common factor was the Lacking. I was on the What's Wrong end of the scales. I didn't trust myself or others. For me to rely on what I would call 'intuition' during these times would be more akin to seeking out a solution that validated my fears and my Lacking. Hence, enter the appearance of a Lacking assumption or judgement that I could easily mistake for intuition.

Intuition is a knowing or understanding that is not based on facts. So the blur between feeling threatened, hurt, fearful, or angry based on joining the dots that are present can easily be dressed up as intuition. The thing is, with intuition, more often than not, the dots don't join in a logical sequence.

It's this difference—the presence of reasons backing up a thought—that I now use as a red flag to help distinguish assumption from intuition.

I also concluded that a strong sense of self and self worth would make the distinction easier and clearer. Self-doubt can plague and cloud one's thinking and view of the world. Self-worth places us closer to the Strength and leaning towards What's Strong. Think about your starting point. Is it What's Wrong or What's Strong in general? Regarding that specific situation?

The Haunted Merry-Go-Round

Have you ever been on a ride that went round in circles and made your head spin so much that the only way to lessen the discomfort was to jump right off? It's these kinds of interactions that I'm talking about—conversations that start as seemingly respectful discussions and seem to go on for far too long into absolute disconnection, disrespect, and lack of boundaries. You may notice this happening with the same people, and it is often about core values. They make you want to slam the phone down or engage in an exchange of essay-length messages or chats in which you feel driven to prove that you are right and they are wrong.

That's when you know you have jumped on a haunted merry-go-round, and your continued engagement is your ticket to ride. Conversely, your safe exit is to simply disembark. This refers to 'It's not you—it's me' because your participation is keeping the battle alive, and your responses or comments are most likely to be leaning towards the elements of the Lacking. Regardless of how it started or who started it.

Of course, when bombarded with comments or ideas that go completely against your core system of beliefs, the reflex can be to defend.

In these kinds of interactions, I generally match the quality of the presenting conversation. So, if an outrageous and offensive claim is made, I could match it with an equally outrageous and offensive claim backing up my position, something that was not only immature but not my usual default.

This calls for an application of the 'It's not you—it's me' principle, in conjunction with:
minding my own business
not taking things personally.

These reminders can help in getting off the haunted merry-go-round. If I feel the need to enter a debate and show that I am right and you are wrong, I am not minding my own business.

If I feel the need to enter a debate and show that I am right and you are wrong, I am taking someone else's views or opinion personally.

What is happening is a competition that puts another's view, opinion, or stance in competition with my own. Competitions are, by nature, designed to extract a winner. The best. The fastest. The biggest. One winner. They have a place and a time—just not when it's a competition that is more like a race to the Lacking at the expense of an individual's self-worth. For when I am confident and secure in my own opinion, I don't feel the need to prove that I am right. I can see myself and others through the lens of the Strength—that's when I won't engage in those merry-go-round conversations.

It just takes one party for the debate to be dismantled, because it does take two to tango.

These reminders work in conjunction with the four guidelines for using the scales with the Self and others.

They also apply to the other party—they have their own role in this haunted merry-go-round, and the same principles could be applied by them. But then again, that's none of your business!

REFLECTION TASK TWENTY-EIGHT

1. Have you ever found yourself in a conversation or chat that launches you into defence or attack mode and seems more like a political debate than a respectful or friendly conversation?
2. Do your responses focus on What's Wrong or What's Strong?
3. Write down a few words to describe how you feel afterwards.
4. Which of the scales would you place your involvement in?
5. Which of the scales would you place the Other's involvement in?
6. Complete the table below with what would be happening in this situation if you applied the guidelines.

Show Forgiveness	Welcome Acceptance	Hold Respect	Apply Love

Applying 'It's not you—it's me' in these situations can be tricky and requires strength, patience, and internal reminders to stay on track. Essentially, it's about reaching a point where you acknowledge that you don't have to be right and can show compassion to the other person even though you might feel that they haven't shown it to you.

It's not you—it's me.

Screen Time

This point goes hand in hand with comparisons, as the online world provides us with an excess of expectations and assumptions from the marketing platforms of those we follow, our online friends, or even the reality TV shows we might watch. Essentially, this could cover anything we watch on a screen.

If watching a screen makes you remember all the things about yourself you dislike or want to change, consider a declutter and refer back to 'It's not you—it's me'.

When logging on to our devices makes us feel like we are in an unhealthy relationship, it can be time for boundaries, or even detox.

My writing journey meant that I had to go online. Initially, it was an exciting new world, and I was enjoying having a digital presence and watching those of others. Yet, as time went by, I became disillusioned with the online world. I came from an offline generation and could remember a time without the internet or mobile phones. I may not have been aware of what was happening on the other side of the world or the latest trend, yet it made absolutely no difference to my life and wellbeing. Sure, seeing a cat push a glass of water off the table is hilarious, but it doesn't stop there.

The reality is that we live in a world driven by money. Many aspects of our life require money to survive in our current society. Most people have to work. Our society has evolved from living in communities to the individual approach—what I need and want—which leans towards the Lacking. The online world can promote this on a global level.

These platforms can have a negative impact on the Self, particularly at times when we are already leaning towards the Lacking. I found that I

was more impacted by screen time when I was in the Lacking mode, which meant I'd interpret and react in a manner that corresponded with my low self-worth at that moment in time. Moving away from the Lacking takes a conscious effort. If that means going offline for a bit, then so be it.
This is done in a way that:

> **shows forgiveness**
> **welcomes acceptance**
> **holds respect**
> **applies love...**

... to both ourselves and the online world

REFLECTION TASK TWENTY-NINE

1. Think about your use of devices and social media. Is there any practice or rule that could be helpful if you feel that your screen usage could be adjusted?
   For example:
   From now on, I will not have my phone by my bed when I am sleeping.
   or
   I will stop screen time at 9:30 p.m.
   or
   Social media only on the weekends.
   or
   No phones during mealtime.

2. Put in place your practice or rule for the next week. After the week, reflect on that time.

3. What was challenging for you?

> 4. What surprised you about it?
> 5. What did you enjoy about it?
> 6. How did you feel about the changes at the beginning of the week? How do you feel about the changes now?
> 7. Do you have any other comments?

Flip it to Faith

For those of you with a particular faith or belief, the Lacking is doubt in the Divine, the Universe, or whomever you worship. So flipping it to faith is saying, 'I trust in you.'

I came to this realisation through the help of an old schoolfriend. Her family was hit with a series of tragedies with a theme of premature loss that merely strengthened the relationship between the two remaining sisters. Sadly, this was to end when one sister died unexpectedly. In the eulogy, my schoolfriend made a powerful statement that filled me with both admiration and awe. I couldn't stop thinking about what she had said as I drove the hour-long trip home with tears streaming from beneath my sunglasses. Her sentiments echoed in my mind long after that day. I couldn't help repeating her words to myself and in many conversations with others soon afterwards.

'God doesn't make mistakes.'

It was such a powerful statement for me because I realised my faith was riddled with doubt, and the reality was that I had absolutely no reason to be going down that track.

'Flip it to faith' became my new mantra, inspired by this old schoolfriend's words of wisdom as she tackled her own pain. In making the flip, faith replaces doubt. In doing so, we:

**show forgiveness
welcome acceptance
hold respect
apply love...**

> **REFLECTION TASK THIRTY**
>
> If this resonates with you, think of a mantra or affirmation that is a meaningful expression of your faith or belief system. Something that embodies and reminds you to flip it to faith. You may also like to refer to a quote or story that is relevant to your belief system. One that encourages or inspires your faith.

As I share this story, I do so having recently finished reading 'The Awakened' Brain by Lisa Miller. This book provides scientific evidence to link spirituality with resilience—the ability to bounce back from adversity. It put forward the idea that living a spiritual life—that is, doing anything that increases one's awareness, regarding both traditional and non-traditional expressions of spirituality, like walking in nature or meditating— has a positive impact on mental health.[43]

I note this here because it adds another layer of meaning to overcoming adversity and the story that I have just shared.

No Regrets

Regrets can all too easily turn a learning opportunity into an opportunity to beat yourself up in a stream of self-doubt in which you might compare yourself to others who did things differently. They may sound like 'I should have' or 'I wished I'd' and imply a lack of faith in one's own decision and abilities.

A wise friend, on many occasions, would gently shut down my expressions of regret in a very simple and compassionate, strengths-based way. She would say:

> *At that time, it was the right decision.*
> *You did your best at that time.*
> *You've learnt so much.*
> *Look at how much you have grown.*
> *In that moment, it was the right thing to do.*

Not only did her advice focus on What's Strong, but it also kept the past in the past.

The challenge is to sit comfortably, to witness with respect, and know and believe that you made the best decision you could have at that time, without applying any of the characteristics of the Lacking to your self-review.

In applying the 'It's not you—it's me' principle here, we place the spotlight on you by exploring your potential lessons from the opportunity that is presenting as regret.

Sometimes, music is the best medicine. Your task here is to listen to, sing, or read the words to Edith Piaf's 'No Regrets' each time you begin to question your actions.[44]

Another method that can help is to be super aware of your choice of words when reflecting on your decisions. A process that can be achieved via elimination.

Eliminating the Word 'Should'

Language is the key here. Any thoughts that indicate regret naturally point to What's Wrong. So, to eliminate the negative impact of regret, rewrite it with the spotlight on What's Strong. The characteristics of the Lacking can provide hints here. Are your sentiments sounding like the Lacking? 'Should have? Could have? I wish I…?'

They are strong verbs that plant the seed of doubt. One way to help negate sentiments of expressly or implied regret is to eliminate the use of the word 'should'. 'I should' implies the Self is in a deficit for doing or not doing things in a particular way.

It might sound like:

I should have known better.
I shouldn't have listened.
I shouldn't have believed her.
I should have…
I shouldn't have…
I should exercise more.
I shouldn't feel angry.
I shouldn't be late.

A rewrite of should—or anything that expresses regret, questions, or doubts about your decisions or actions—is achieved through the exploration of the reason those sentiments are important. How? By simply and repeatedly asking, 'Why?'

For example:
The should: I shouldn't have listened to her.
Why?
It's important to me that I make my own decisions.
Why?
It's important to me because I feel empowered.
Why?
It's important that I have confidence in and value myself.

> **REFLECTION TASK THIRTY-ONE**
>
> 1. Write down an 'I should/shouldn't' or 'I wish I'd' sentence that is relevant to you.
>   For example:
>   *'I shouldn't be late'.*
>
> 2. Think about why this is important to you and rewrite, starting with 'It's important to me that…' followed by a strengths-based reason. It may help to think about the associated benefit.
>   *'It's important to me that I am on time.'*
>
> 3. Now go back to your new sentence and again consider the 'why' behind it.
>   'It's important to me that I am on time.'
>   Why?
>   *'It's important to me that I do what I say I am going to do.'*
>
> 4. If you are still up for some more, you can again ask why.
>   'It's important to me that I do what I say I am going to do.'
>   Why?
>   *'It's important that I show integrity, honesty, and respect for others.'*
>
> 5. Reflect on your answers. What do you notice?

The key message from this book is the importance and impact that our thoughts have on our lived experience. The quality of our thoughts will be reflected in our physical world, and conversely, our physical world will give us clues as to whether our thoughts lean predominately towards What's Wrong or What's Strong. At times, this connection is not obvious, as there are and will continue to be times where an external factor can be linked to the main cause of life not going as planned. It's true; external factors do impact our lives, and how we respond—that is always our choice. I know this is confronting and will challenge some. That is what led me to seek out known examples of those who overcame adversity. These examples really confirmed for me that our thoughts, intangible as they are, can and do enact physical change.

Not only can they materialise in our day-to-day living, but the science verified that our thoughts or mental experience could change the structure of our brains.

The value, importance, and impact of the quality of our thoughts will be reflected in what we do, say, and feel, in addition to our thoughts. This multidimensional aspect of our mental experience is where we can obtain the physical clues that will help highlight which lens is being applied.

Along with this multidimensional aspect, we saw the dualities in play.

Duality number one showed us the hidden lessons that can be found in polar opposites. Did we lean towards What's Wrong or What's Strong? This is a concept that could also be broken down by exploring what is happening as well as the opposite of what is happening—what is not happening.

The second duality introduced us to the characters, as there are always two: the Self, and essentially everybody else—the Other. This provides another way to further break down our self-talk and interactions.

'It's not you—it's me!' is a companion to self-reflection and growth in which the spotlight is shifted inwards. This process that has no real beginning or end; it is continual and can be challenging. I stress the importance and value of our thoughts; this includes the lens we use to view our self-reflection and growth process. It's less about staying on the side of the Strength or What's Strong most of the time and more about how quickly and smoothly we can stand back and acknowledge that we were in the Lacking and readjust and be ready to practise applying these discoveries to future opportunities that will arise. What's important is that the lessons learnt are taken on board and practised. Sometimes, we need more life examples of the Lacking to see and realise the valuable lessons. Other times, the lessons might arise sooner. The timeframe will be unique to each individual and situation. I encourage you to apply the What's Strong lens to this process and celebrate your progress and achievements.

For those times when progress might be stagnant, or you see repeat situations occurring, ones that you aren't proud of or lean you further into the Lacking and What's Wrong, this is where I encourage you to consider applying the guidelines to those conversations with yourself. You know the conversations I'm referring to—self-criticism, rumination, over-thinking, jumping to negative conclusions—those kinds of dialogues that take up a lot of time and energy. Apply these guidelines to those conversations:

show forgiveness
welcome acceptance
hold respect
apply love...

Where we place our focus will be the direction that our physical experience forms and takes, yet where we place our focus has complex origins and contributing factors. Your journey may, at times, feel like you are going full speed ahead, while other times it may feel like you are walking backwards or standing still. Regardless of the speed or pace of your journey, it is yours and yours alone. Embrace it. Celebrate it. Forgive it. Practise it. Learn from it. Discover it. Acknowledge it. Accept it.

It won't always be easy or straightforward, but your consistent effort will pay off, and you will reap the rewards that flow, as your reality will be a reflection of your thoughts.

You will be challenged, sometimes in unexpected ways.

Remember those who overcame adversity and triumphed in almost unimaginable ways; let their stories inspire you and know that you have your own story in the making, one that will offer up a range of opportunities and chapters for you to write and rewrite as your story evolves. These are stories that you will reread with fond memories and a sense of achievement as you celebrate the progress you have created.

More importantly, keep the spotlight on you, your destination, your goals, your interest, and your life. When the spotlight deviates, just remember all the times you kept the light shining brightly on you as you readjust the spotlight so that it illuminates the Strength in you.

BIBLIOGRAPHY

Aron E. (2015). The highly sensitive child: helping our children thrive when the world overwhelms them. Broadway Books, New York.

Aron E. (2015). The highly sensitive child: helping our children thrive when the world overwhelms them. Broadway Books, New York.

Bentzen M, Hagen K, and Worre Foged J (2018) The neuroaffective picture book: an illustrated introduction to developmental neuropsychology, North Atlantic Books, Berkeley.

Bernet W., Wamboldt M. Z., and Narrow W. E. (2016). Child Affected by Parental relationship stress Journal of the American Academy of Child and Adolescent Psychiatry, 55(7): 571–579.

Centre on the Developing Child (2010) The Foundations of Lifelong Health Are Built in Early Childhood, accessed on November 7, 2021.

<www.developingchild.harvard.edu/resources/the-foundations-of-lifelong-health-are-built-in-early-childhood/>.

Cozolino L. (29th July–3rd August 2018) 'The Social Brain', conference presentation: Third International Childhood Trauma Conference, Melbourne. <https://vimeo.com/291853211>.

Dalai Lama (19 September 2017), Io Sono [Panel Discussion] Festival delle Religioni, Florence.
< https://youtu.be/25rERneeELU.

Doidge, N. (2016). The brain's way of healing: stories of remarkable re-coveries and discoveries, Penguin Books, London.

Bibliography

Doidge, N. (2007). The brain that changes itself: Stories of personal Triumph from the Frontiers of Brain Science, Scribe, Melbourne.

Donne J, (1624) Devotions upon Emergent Occasions, Meditation XVII.

Engel B, (2002), The Power of Anger: Healing Steps to Transform All Your Relationships, Wiley, New York.

Evidence Act 1995 NSW Chapter 3.

Felitti VJ, Anda RF, Nordenberg D, Williamson DF, Spitz AM, Edwards V, Koss MP, & Marks JS (1998), 'Relationship of Childhood Abuse and Household Dysfunction to Many of the Leading Causes of Death in Adults: The Adverse Childhood Experiences (ACE) Study', American Journal of Preventive Medicine, 14(4):245-258, DOI: 10.1016/s0749-3797(98)00017-8.

Fisher R, Ury W, and Patton B (1991) Getting to Yes: Negotiating agreement without giving in, 2nd edn., Penguin, New York.

Fletcher D (Director) (2019), Rocketman (Film), Paramount Pictures, United States.

Golding W, (1954) Lord of the Flies, Coles, Toronto.

Harvard Study (2015) Harvard Second Generation Study, accessed on November 7, 2022. <https://www.adultdevelopmentstudy.org/>.

Hölzel BK, Carmody J, Vangel M, Congleton C, Yerramsetti SM, Gard T, and Lazar SW, mindfulness practice leads to increases in regional brain gray matter density. Psychiatry Research:

Neuroimaging, 191(1), pp. 36–43. 2011. <doi.org/10.1016/j.pscychres-ns.2010.08.006>.

Bibliography

Karakochu CD, Whitfield KC, Green TJ, and Kraemer J (2017), The biology of the first 1000 days, CRC Press, Boca Raton.

Kerr ME & Bowen M (1988), Family evaluation: An approach based on Bowen theory, W W Norton & Co. New York.

Kübler-Ross E and Kessle D, (2014) On grief & grieving: finding the meaning of grief through the five stages of loss, Simon & Schuster Uk Ltd, London.

Lazar SW, Kerr CE, Wasserman RH, Gray JR, Greve DN, Treadway MT, McGarvey M, Quinn BT, Dusek JA, Benson H, Rauch SL, Moore CI, and Fischl B, (2005) Meditation experience is associated with increased cortical thickness. Neuroreport, 16(17):1893–7.

<www.ncbi.nlm.nih.gov/pmc/articles/PMC1361002/>.

Lebow J, Chambers A, and Breunlin DC, Encyclopedia of Couple and Family Therapy, Springer International Publishing, Cham.

Lebow J, Chambers A, and Breunlin DC, (2019) Encyclopedia of Couple and Family Therapy, Springer International Publishing, Cham.

Lieberman MD and Eisenberger NI, (2009) Pains and Pleasures of Social Life, Science, 323(5916):890–891, doi.org/10.1126/science.1170008.

Lipton BH, (2006) The Wisdom of Your Cells: How your beliefs control your biology, Sounds True, Boulder.

Magrini M, (2019) The brain: a user's manual: a simple guide to the world's most complex machine, Short Books, London.

Bibliography

Mccashen W, (2017) The strengths approach: sharing power, building hope, creating change (2nd ed), Victoria: St Luke's Innovative Resources.

Megginson LC, (1963) Lessons from Europe for American Business, The Southwestern Social Science Quarterly 44(1): 3–13.

<www.jstor.org/stable/4286693>.

Miller L, (2021) The awakened brain: the psychology of spirituality and our search for meaning, Allen Lane, London.

Monk G and Winslade J, (2013) Practicing Narrative Mediation, Jossey-Bass, San Francisco.

Moore TG, Arefadib N, Deery A, Keyes M & West S, (2017) The First Thousand Days: An Evidence Paper – Summary, Centre for Community Child Health, Murdoch Children's Research Institute, Parkville.

Mukherjee S, (2016) The gene: an intimate history, Scribner, New York.

Myerscough J (Director), 2018, The Placebo Experiment: Can My Brain Cure My Body. (Documentary) Windfalls Films, United Kingdom.

National Scientific Council on the Developing Child (2010). Early Experiences Can Alter Gene Expression and Affect Long-Term Development: Working Paper No. 10.
<www.developingchild.harvard.edu>.

Nelson CA, Fox NA, and Zeanah CH, (2014) Romania's abandoned children: deprivation, brain development, and the struggle for recovery, Cambridge, Harvard University Press, Cambridge.

Bibliography

Pittman CM and Karle EM, (2016) Rewire your anxious brain: how to use the neuroscience of fear to end anxiety, panic and worry, New Harbinger Publications, Oakland.

Porges SW, (29th July-3rd August 2018) Understanding trauma through the lens of the polyvagal theory. [conference presentation] Third International Childhood Trauma Conference, Melbourne. <https:// vimeo.com/372785332>.

Porges SW, (2017) The pocket guide to polyvagal theory: the transformative power of feeling safe, W.W Norton & Company, New York.

Porges SW, (17th-20th August 2017) Vagal Pathways: Portals to Compassion and Presence, [conference presentation] 11th Annual Swiss Learning Festival: Presence and Compassion, Weggis. <www.bildungsfestival.ch/en/bildungsfestival>.

Rozin P and Royzman EB, (2001) Negativity Bias, Negativity Dominance, and Contagion, Personality and Social Psychology Review, 5(4):296-320, DOI:10.1207/S15327957PSPR0504_2

Schwartz J and Begley S, (2007) The mind and the brain : neuroplasticity and the power of mental force, Harper Collins, New York.

Siegel DJ, (2010) The mindful therapist : a clinician's guide to mind- sight and neural integration, Norton & Co, New York.

Siegel RD, (2014) The Science of Mindfulness: a Research- Based Path to Well-Being. The Great Courses, Virginia.

Steiner R and Bamford C, (2004) Start now! a book of soul and spiritual exercises, Steinerbooks, Great Barrington.

Bibliography

Teicher MH, (6th-10th June 2016) Child abuse, Brain development and Psychopathology, [conference presentation] Second International Childhood Trauma Conference, Melbourne. <https://vimeo.com/314151321>.

Tronick E, (2007) The neurobehavioral and social- emotional development of infants and children, W. W. Norton & Co, New York.

Vaillant GE, (2012) Triumphs of Experience; The Men of the Harvard Grant Study, The Belknap Press of Harvard University Press, Cambridge MA.

van der Kolk BA, McFarlane AC and Weisæth L, (2017) Traumatic stress: the effects of overwhelming experience on mind, body and society, Guilford Press, New York.

Vaucaire M, (1963) No regrets, (song) Columbia.

Wallis N, (25th July 2019) The developing brain-impact on anxiety, autism and depression, [presentation] Autism Advisory and Support Service, Sydney.

Westrupp EM, Rose N, Nicholson J and Brow S, (2015) Exposure to inter-parental conflict across 10 years of childhood: data from the longitudinal study of Australian children, Maternal and Child Health Journal, 19(9):1966–1973, doi: 10.1007/s10995-015-1704-3.

Westrupp EM, Brown S, Woolhouse H, Gartland D and Nicholson JM, (2014) Repeated early-life exposure to inter-parental conflict increases risk of preadolescent mental health problems, European Journal of Pediatrics, 177(3):419–427, doi:10.1007/s00431-017-3071-0.

Wilson RZ, (2014) Neuroscience for counsellors: practical applications for counsellors, therapists and mental health practitioners, Jessica Kingsley Publishers, London.

Wolynn M. (2017) It didn't start with you: how inherited family trauma shapes who we are and how to end the cycle, Penguin Books, New York.

Yehuda R, Daskalakis NP, Bierer LM, Bader HN, Klengel T, Holsboer F, and Binder EB (2016), Holocaust Exposure Induced Intergenerational Effects on FKBP5 Methylation, Biological Psychiatry, 80(5):372–380, doi:10.1016/j.biopsych.2015.08.005.

REFERENCES

1 Fletcher D (Director) (2019), Rocketman (Film) Paramount Pictures, United States.

2 Kübler-Ross E. and Kessle D. (2014). On grief and grieving: finding the meaning of grief through the five stages of loss. Simon & Schuster UK Ltd., London.

3 Mccashen W. (2017), The Strengths Approach: Sharing Power, Building Hope, and Creating Change (2nd ed.), Victoria: St. Luke's Innovative Resources.

4 Monk G. and Winslade J. (2013), Practicing Narrative Mediation, Jossey-Bass, San Francisco.

5 Fisher R., Ury W., and Patton B. (1991), Getting to Yes: Negotiating an Agreement Without Giving in, 2nd edn., Penguin, New York.

6 Porges SW (17th–20th August 2017) Vagal Pathways: Portals to Compassion and Presence [conference presentation] 11th Annual Swiss Learning Festival: Presence and Compassion, Weggis. <www.bildungsfestival.ch/en/bildungsfestival>.

7 Evidence Act 1995 NSW, Chapter 3.

8 Bentzen M, Hagen K, and Worre Foged J (2018) The neuroaffective picture book: an illustrated introduction to developmental neuropsychology, North Atlantic Books, Berkeley.

9 Magrini M. (2019), The Brain: A user's Manual: A simple Guide to the World's Most Complex Machine, Short Books, London.

References

10 Golding W. (1954), Lord of the Flies, Coles, Toronto.

11 Rozin P. and Royzman EB (2001), Negativity Bias, Negativity Dominance, and Contagion. Personality and Social Psychology Review, 5(4)296-320, DOI:10.1207/S15327957PSPR0504_2.

12 Megginson LC (1963), 'Lessons from Europe for American Business', The Southwestern Social Science Quarterly, vol. 44, no. 1, 3–13. www.jstor.org/stable/42866937.

13 Porges SW, (2017), The Pocket Guide to Polyvagal Theory: The Transformative Power of Feeling Safe, W.W. Norton & Company, New York.

14 Magrini M. (2019), The Brain: A user's Manual: A simple Guide to the World's Most Complex Machine, Short Books, London.

15 Donne J. (1642), Devotions upon Emergent Occasions, Meditation XVII. Originally published in 1624.

16 Lemov RM (2006). World as Laboratory: Experiments with Mice, Mazes, and Men, Hill and Wang, New York.

17 Nelson CA, Fox NA, and Zeanah CH, Romania's abandoned children: deprivation, brain development, and the struggle for recovery, Cambridge, Harvard University Press, 2014.

18 Tronick E. (2007). The neurobehavioral and social-emotional development of infants and children, W. W. Norton & Co., New York.

19 Vaillant, Triumphs of Experience: The Men of the Harvard Grant Study, The Belknap Press of Harvard University Press, Cambridge, MA, 2012.

References

20 Magrini M., The Brain: A user's Manual: A simple Guide to the World's Most Complex Machine, London, Short Books, 2019.

21 Moore TG, Arefadib N, Deery A, Keyes M, and West S, The First Thousand Days: An Evidence Paper—Summary. Parkville, Victoria: Centre for Community Child Health, Murdoch Children's Research Institute, 2017.

22 Felitti VJ, Anda RF, Nordenberg D, Williamson DF, Spitz AM, Edwards V, Koss MP, & Marks JS, 'Relationship of Childhood Abuse and Household Dysfunction to Many of the Leading Causes of Death in Adults: The Adverse Childhood Experiences (ACE) Study', American Journal of Preventive Medicine, vol. 56, no. 6, 1998.

23 Magrini, The Brain: A user's Manual: A simple Guide to the World's Most Complex Machine, London, Short Books, 2019.

24 Lieberman MD, and Eisenberger NI, 'NEUROSCIENCE: Pains and Pleasures of Social Life'. Science, 323(5916), pp. 890–891, 2009.

25 Doidge, N. (2007). The brain that changes itself: Stories of Personal Triumph from the Frontiers of Brain Science, Scribe, Melbourne.

26 Ibid., pp. 200–202.

27 Myerscough (Director), 2018, The Placebo Experiment: Can My Brain Cure My Body. (Documentary) Windfalls Films.

28 Westrupp E, Rose N, Nicholson J, Brow S, 'Exposure to inter-parental conflict across 10 years of childhood: data from the longitudinal study of Australian children'. Maternal and Child Health Journal, 19:1966–1973, 2015.

References

29 Bernet W, Wamboldt MZ, and Narrow WE, 'Child Affected by Parental Relationship Distress'. Journal of the American Academy of Child and Adolescent Psychiatry, 55(7), pp. 571–579, 2016.

30 Aron E., The highly sensitive child: helping our children thrive when the world overwhelms them, New York, Broadway Books, 2015.

31 van der Kolk BA, McFarlane AC, and Weisæth L, Traumatic stress: the effects of overwhelming experience on mind, body, and society, New York, Guilford Press, 2017.

32 Wilson RZ, Neuroscience for Counsellors: Practical applications for counsellors, therapists, and mental health practitioners, London, Jessica Kingsley Publishers, 2014.

33 Teicher MH, Samson JA, Anderson CM, and Ohashi K, The effects of childhood maltreatment on brain structure, function, and connectivity. Nature Reviews Neuroscience, 17(10), pp. 652–666, 2016.

34 Mukherjee S. (2016), The Gene: An Intimate History, Scribner, New York.

35 Kerr EM & Bowen M (1988), Family evaluation: An approach based on Bowen theory, W. W. Norton & Co., 1988.

36 Lebow J., A. Chambers, and D. C. Breunlin, Encyclopaedia of Couple and Family Therapy, Cham, Springer International Publishing, 2019.

37 Westrupp EM, S Brown S, Woolhouse H, Gartland D, and J M Nicholson, Repeated early-life exposure to inter-parental Conflict increases the risk of preadolescent mental health problems. European Journal of Paediatrics, 177(3), pp. 419–427, 2017.

References

38 Lazar SW, Kerr CE, Wasserman RH, Grey JR, Greve DN, Treadway MT, McGarvey M, Quinn BT, Dusek JA, Benson H, Rauch SL, Moore CI, and Fischl B (2005) The meditation experience is associated with increased cortical thickness. Neuroreport, [online] 16(17), pp. 1893–7, 2005, <www.ncbi.nlm.nih.gov/pmc/articles/PMC1361002/>.

39 Steiner R. and Bamford C. (2004) Start now! a book of soul and spiritual exercises: meditation instructions, Steinerbooks, Great Barrington.

40 Evidence Act 1995 NSW Chapter 3.

41 Wolynn M. (2017) It didn't start with you: how inherited family trauma shapes who we are and how to end the cycle, Penguin Books, New York.

42 Yehuda R, Daskalakis NP, Bierer LM, Bader HN, Klengel T, Holsboer F. and Binder EB, Holocaust Exposure Induced Intergenerational Effects on FKBP5 Methylation. Biological Psychiatry, [online] 80(5), pp.372–380, 2016.
www.sciencedirect.com/science/article/pii S0006322315006526.

43 Miller, L. (2021). The awakened brain: the psychology of spirituality and our search for meaning, Allen Lane, London.

44 Vaucaire M. (1963), No regrets, (song) Columbia.

About The Author

Rosemary Gattuso is an alternate dispute resolution practitioner specialising in family mediation and restorative justice practices.

As a family dispute resolution practitioner, she has helped many families to separate respectfully and in a child-focused way and is on various Restorative Justice panels for Commonwealth agencies.

Her practice draws on being present with clients as they navigate the changes and challenges that confront them in a trauma-informed and strengths-based way.

As a facilitator, she has been able to share her knowledge and experience on a larger scale, assisting mediators and mental health practitioners to work with a strengths-based lens.

Her interest and continued professional development in child development, trauma and neuroscience have added another layer of meaning to the way in which she works and has placed her in a unique position to observe, learn, reflect and share.

Rosemary holds a strong academic record, encompassing both undergraduate and postgraduate law, couples and family therapy and family dispute resolution. Her initial interest in mediation sparked during her undergraduate studies and prompted her to pursue advanced studies in mediation and negotiation at Harvard University.

She regularly runs workshops and information sessions on trauma-informed living and strengths-based practices in high schools, businesses and with mental health practitioners to enhance resilience and mindful introspection.

As a chronic over-thinker, Rosemary experienced first-hand the transformative impact of rewriting overthinking into strengths-based

About The Author

reflection and is committed to sharing this with the world.

Rosemary resides in Sydney, Australia. To learn more, please visit www.rosemarygattuso.com

Notes

Notes

HELIX PRESS

ISBN: 978-0-6456080-0-7

First Edition 2024

© Copyright 2024 Rosemary Gattuso
Designed and created In Australia